D0321619

Language for Learning Mathematics
Assessment for Learning in Practice

Clare Lee

Open University Press

Open University Press
McGraw-Hill Education
McGraw-Hill House
Shoppenhangers Road
Maidenhead, Berkshire
England SL6 2QL

email: enquiries@openup.co.uk
world wide web: www.openup.co.uk

and Two Penn Plaza, New York, NY 1012–2289 USA

First published 2006

Copyright © Clare Lee 2006

All rights reserved. Except for the quotation of short passages for the purpose of criticism and review, no part of this publication may be reproduced, stored in a retrieval system, or transmitted, in any form or by any means, electronic, mechanical, photocopying, recording or otherwise, without the prior written permission of the publisher or a licence from the Copyright Licensing Agency Limited. Details of such licences (for reprographic reproduction) may be obtained from the Copyright Licensing Agency Limited of 90 Tottenham Court Road, London W1T 4LP.

A catalogue record of this book is available from the British Library

ISBN-10: 0 335 21988 8 (pb)   0 335 21989 6 (hb)
ISVN-13: 978 0 335 21988 9 (pb)   978 0 335 21989 6 (hb)

Library of Congress Cataloging-in-Publication Data
CIP data has been applied for

Typeset by BookEns Ltd, Royston, Herts.
Printed and bound in Poland by OZGraf. S.A.

Contents

Acknowledgements

I acknowledge with thanks the work of the many teachers and colleagues in Warwickshire and beyond who have worked with me to reveal what the ideas this book contains mean in practice. Thank you for your time and your willingness to try out ideas, to discuss and to debate. Thank you for your support.

Thanks also go to Barbara, whose unfailing belief and wisdom supported me in developing my knowledge, and, of course, to my husband.

How this book tells its story

This book contains seven chapters, which I have arranged so that they build ideas from one chapter to the next. However, some people will want to use the book for different purposes and, therefore, use some chapters more than others. The book has three distinct strands: an overview of mathematical language and learning, the theoretical background to the ideas and the practical implementation of those ideas.

Chapters 1 and 7 give an overview to the ideas. Chapter 1 introduces both the coverage of the book and how the ideas were developed through action research. Chapter 7 concludes by summing up the aims of the ideas and their significance and the key ideas in making sustained changes in professional practice.

Chapters 2 and 6 explore the theoretical background. Chapter 2 investigates and explains what mathematical language is, using the available literature to set out what pupils must learn in order to be able to use mathematical language to express their ideas and use and control mathematical concepts. Chapter 6 looks more deeply at the literature surrounding language use and mathematical learning. It explores both the background to focusing on language and communication skills in order to aid learning and instigate Assessment for Learning, and the specific effect that such a focus can be expected to have on pupils' mathematical learning. It also explores some theoretical aspects of change and how action research contributes to developing professional knowledge.

Chapters 3, 4 and 5 are the heart of the book, describing how the ideas can be implemented in mathematical classrooms and how the focus on language intertwines with ideas about developing Assessment for Learning. Chapter 3 discusses the basics of getting started in focusing on language in a classroom. Chapter 4 discusses Assessment for Learning and how its potential for improved learning can be used effectively in a talking and learning mathematics classroom. Chapter 5 continues the practical focus, exploring further ideas for involving the pupils in the talking and the learning process.

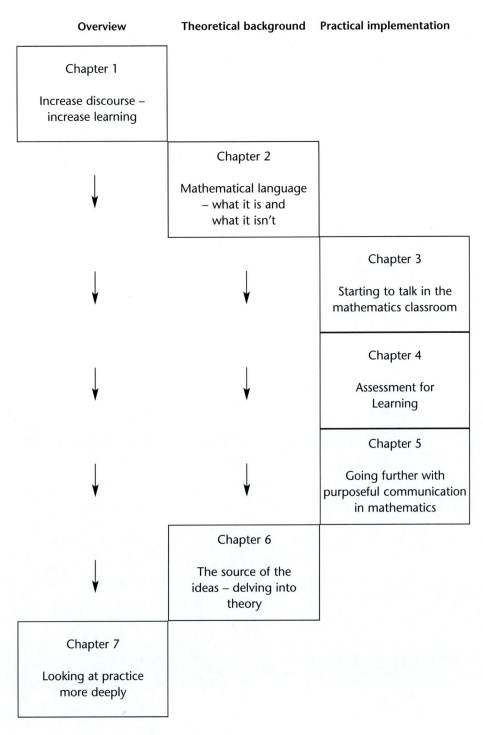

Occasionally I introduce quotes in italics. These come from classrooms where I have been the teacher or the observer, or from teachers with whom I have worked. There are also boxes that contain short descriptions of named pupils and some of the evidence for asserting that discourse helped them to develop their mathematical knowledge.

1 Increase discourse – increase learning

This book is essentially about increasing the amount of discourse that takes place in a mathematics classroom. There are many reasons this is a good idea, as I will explain as the book continues. However, the chief reason that increasing discourse is important is that it increases the potential for the pupils to learn mathematics and for teachers to help their pupils learn. When you increase the amount of discourse in which the pupils engage, the meaning of words and ideas can be negotiated and extended, and both teacher and pupils can decide on the best way forward with the learning. Once the pupils are engaged in articulating their ideas, Assessment for Learning becomes an embedded part of classroom practice.

I use the word 'discourse' a great deal in this book. By 'discourse' I mean the full range of language use that can be entered into in a classroom. In order to learn mathematics effectively, pupils primarily need to talk about their mathematical ideas, negotiate meanings, discuss ideas and strategies and make mathematical language their own. However, talk is ephemeral and the discipline of writing can make ephemeral thoughts more permanent and, therefore, more easily remembered at a later date. The term 'discourse' also indicates that the pupils are involved in this process; they do the negotiating and discussing, they transform their transient ideas into permanent writing. The teacher initiates and shares in the discourse and manages a process that enables the pupils to become more and more proficient in continuing the discourse. The pupils learn to take part in mathematical discourse and in the process learn to use and control mathematical ideas; they become successful learners of mathematics.

Discourse and Assessment for Learning

Increasing the amount of discourse in a mathematics classroom will increase the use of Assessment for Learning in that classroom. Effective learning and Assessment for Learning – formative assessment – are intimately connected, as has been explained in other publications (Black *et al.* 2002, 2003). If the amount of mathematical language that the pupils use is increased then, among many other benefits, Assessment for Learning can be used effectively, which will, in and of itself, increase the pupils' learning. Therefore, this book is about stimulating increased use of mathematics language by the pupils *and* it is about practical ways to use Assessment for Learning in mathematics, because one leads to the other. Increasing the pupils' ability to use mathematical language means that both the pupils themselves and their teachers can explore their understanding of mathematical concepts and, therefore, either pupil or teacher, or both, will be in a position to act to extend that understanding. It is in acting to extend understanding that the exploration becomes formative assessment and learning is increased.

Mathematical language – a barrier to overcome

Using mathematical language can be a barrier to pupils' learning because of particular requirements and conventions in expressing mathematical ideas. Pupils do need to learn to express their mathematical ideas; teachers cannot expect them to be able to do this without help. For many pupils, learning to use language to express mathematical ideas will be similar to learning to speak a foreign language. Pupils have to learn specific vocabulary, but also means of expression and phrasing that are specifically mathematical and which make it possible to explain mathematical ideas. Unless the pupils know about the way that language is used in mathematics they may think that they do not understand a certain concept when what they cannot do is express the idea in language. Conversely, being able to express their mathematical ideas clearly enables pupils to know that they understand and can use mathematical ideas. Teachers will extend their pupils' ability to learn mathematics by helping them to express their ideas using appropriate language and by recognizing that they need to use language in a way that is different from their everyday use.

Increase mathematical discourse, increase learning

Pupils expressing their own mathematical ideas has many benefits, all of which are intertwined with Assessment for Learning. Once pupils can articulate their ideas they can 'talk through' a problem and can transform the original idea to fit new circumstances. Pupils' ability to articulate their mathematical ideas as they learn enables them to take control of these ideas and transfer them to other situations. They can consider the appropriateness of applying the ideas, try out new ways of using them, take wrong turnings, which they can then assess for themselves, and thereby explore alternative solutions. The ability to talk about ideas gives the pupils the potential to be efficient mathematical problem solvers, and thereby enables them to take on more challenging work. Because the pupils can express their ideas they can control how they use them in ways that tacit learning does not allow.

Pupils and their teacher can become confident of the pupils' understanding when they can express their ideas. Pupils that are able to talk about their mathematical learning can articulate for themselves what else they need to learn. They know what mathematical ideas they can use and can express where to improve their learning. The teacher is able to listen to what the pupils really know, to assess for misunderstandings or for where learning needs to be extended. When the pupils have been taught to use mathematical language to express their ideas the teacher no longer has to 'guess' at the state of the pupils' learning but can act to extend that learning appropriately. Pupils who regularly work to articulate their ideas and understandings can deal with ideas that are usually considered challenging for their age group. They have confidence that they can deal with mathematical ideas and are therefore willing to push at the boundaries of the work they are offered.

Increasing discourse in the classroom will mean that meanings are shared within that classroom. When names are used in mathematics they often convey a complex web of ideas. Consider, for example, the term 'rectangle', indicating a two-dimensional figure with four right angles, four sides and two pairs of parallel lines. Pupils are often asked to consider ideas about the relative length of the sides of a rectangle or that the diagonals cross in the centre of the figure but may not be perpendicular, and so on. A rectangle is a very simple figure but pupils will become aware of an increasing number of associated concepts as they learn more about mathematics. Therefore, the term 'rectangle' will indicate to pupils an increasingly complex web of ideas. When the pupils are involved in the discussion and negotiation meanings are shared. Too often the teacher uses specific mathematical language but the pupils do not. If the pupils do not take a full part in the discourse then they will not 'share' the meaning but instead will have received it, which is not the same thing. Pupils are often reluctant to use mathematical words. Mathematical expressions are not 'their words' but rather words that are used by a community of people that they do not feel part of, and often do not see a way to become part of. It is one of the mathematics teacher's jobs to help her/his pupils bridge this divide. When teachers act to help pupils use essential words and phraseology to express mathematical ideas, they enable the pupils to take part in a learning discourse.

The benefits of pupils' involvement in mathematical discourse

Articulating mathematical ideas

Asking pupils to articulate their current understanding of a mathematical idea enables them to become aware of, develop and reorganize their knowledge. Articulating their ideas helps pupils to remember what they have worked with and makes the knowledge available for them to use and control. They learn mathematical concepts. When pupils articulate their ideas they see themselves as being able to solve mathematical problems.

Being involved in mathematical discourse involves assigning meanings to words and phrases which are shared within a community. If all members of the class take a part in the discourse then everyone shares the meanings generated. Taking a full part in the discourse means that pupils articulate their own ideas, as well as listen to and reflect on ideas that others express. The teacher will also share in these meanings and will therefore have access to pupils' understandings and misunderstandings. The teacher can then modify the teaching activities in the classroom to meet pupils' actual learning needs; that is, they will be able to use formative assessment.

Challenge

When the pupils are engaged in using mathematical discourse more challenging work can be undertaken. Taking part in mathematical discourse enables the pupils to have confidence in what they can do and understand. They know when they have successfully understood concepts and are prepared to use those ideas to solve challenging problems. In order to raise pupils' attainment in mathematics the level of challenge in the work that pupils are asked to do must be as high as possible, without causing them to lose hope of being able to comprehend. Involving pupils in mathematical discourse means that the teacher can be sure that the challenge level is as high possible and the pupils can know that they are learning effectively.

Involving the pupils in the learning process

Discourse enables pupils to be involved in the learning process. This is a primary factor in using Assessment for Learning. When pupils feel involved in the learning process they will be more responsible, more self-efficacious and ultimately more successful. However, to be involved in the learning process in mathematics they must be able to express their ideas and discuss and negotiate with one another; that is, they must be able to use mathematical language.

Part of being involved in the learning process consists of taking some responsibility for the outcome of that process. When pupils take on such responsibility they see the teacher as a resource to help their learning, not as the *only* person who knows what should be done. Discourse in the class can be about the content that the pupils are to learn and also, importantly, about the way that they may learn effectively. When the pupils take a full part in discussions, affecting the course of the discussion and being affected by it, they go away from it able to use the ideas discussed.

Pupils also become involved in the learning process by being offered choice and being allowed, and encouraged, to make decisions about the work that they do and the way that the learning process proceeds. Pupils welcome choice in the way that they continue with their learning, although they may take some time to become accustomed to being allowed to make their own choices. Pupils also become involved in the learning process by being part of the teaching process. When pupils help one another to learn about mathematical ideas they naturally take on the identity of someone who can 'do' mathematics.

Pupils' involvement in the learning process means that they became an integral part of a discourse that develops knowledge; they became part of a meaning-making, discourse community. They can take a meta-cognitive stance, becoming aware of their own learning and beginning to take responsibility for it.

Communities outside the classroom

It is self-evident that the wider community of the school has a great effect on what goes on within the classroom. The effects may be overt – for example, the norms of pupils sitting in rows and not talking during lessons – or subtle – such as pupils' expectations of both their behaviour and the teacher's within a lesson. The pupils may expect not to be involved in the lesson, to have everything organized for them and the teaching 'done to' them. Asking such pupils to think and express their ideas can be a struggle. It would be helpful if the whole school changed its approach and decided to stimulate language use and increased thinking and reflection as part of, say, a drive to improve literacy in the school. However, the lack of a whole-school focus is not a reason to neglect these issues. I know of many mathematics classrooms where pupils articulate and justify their ideas and generate meanings regardless of what happens in other lessons.

Sometimes the whole of society seems to be conspiring against the talking, learning mathematics classroom. Pupils come to mathematics lessons with the idea that there is one right way to solve any mathematics problem and one right answer to that problem. Pupils are often reluctant to give alternative ideas once one has been given. This is understandable as, from their view, all but one answer must be incorrect. These ideas can be overcome in time and with the different approaches advocated in the later chapters. Pupils are often overly concerned about not making mistakes and sometimes would rather do nothing than commit to what might be an erroneous idea. Such feelings stop pupils taking a full part in the discourse. They are reluctant to negotiate or to contribute to a discussion because they are concerned about making a mistake or giving a wrong answer.

Assessment for Learning has a large contribution to make in overcoming this huge barrier to learning in mathematics. First, setting out the learning objectives for the lesson clarifies exactly what and how the pupils are intended to learn. Peer and self-assessment can help build an idea of all the shades and nuances that amount to a high-quality outcome of the learning process. Pupils can use this process to build a confident knowledge that they are 'doing it right' even when their work is different from their peers. Such approaches can help pupils have confidence in their ability to know the required outcome of their work and that they can keep themselves on the right track.

Many pupils come to the classroom with the idea that they have a predetermined and fixed level of ability. In mathematics they are often worried that this level is low. This is an 'entity theory of learning' (Dweck 2000) and is prevalent in much of society. The idea that pupils have a fixed level of ability in mathematics may have been reinforced by 'setting' or 'grouping' procedures in schools, but in other ways as well. The approaches that I am advocating depend on the idea that everyone can become better able to use mathematical ideas by addressing the particular difficulties in learning that they have (the incremental theory of learning). This may be a new idea to the pupils. If, in the past, a pupil had frequently tried and failed to learn mathematics, it is unsurprising if he or she gives up trying. In these circumstances the choice for pupils may seem to be between appearing to be lazy and not trying, or trying and giving the impression of being stupid. It seems, on balance, to be a sensible decision when pupils decide that they would rather be thought lazy than stupid. It is important to emphasize in teaching the incremental view of learning; everyone can improve with perseverance from themselves and help and support from others.

Making connections in mathematics

Increased discourse in the classroom has the potential to help pupils make connections between areas of mathematical learning. In school classrooms, mathematics tends to be taught in a segmented fashion. The lessons are planned under headings: fractions, Pythagoras' theorem, probability, the 'Golf Ball Project', and so on. Pupils will see each set of lessons as quite different from the others unless their teacher takes steps to help them to appreciate the links and connections between them. Mathematics is a series of interconnected ideas; every mathematical area – algebra, geometry, trigonometry, and so on – is part of a whole that constitutes an evolving system, a way of thinking and communicating ideas. Pupils contribute to the system when they generalize or formalize, when they look for patterns or consistency. I would argue that these generic skills – generalizing, searching for patterns, and so on – are ultimately more important to the pupils than, for example, being able to state Pythagoras' theorem, although that would be useful as well. The pupils' view of mathematics tends to be that it consists of patterns and diagrams, and they begin to show an appreciation of symbolic language, explanation, reasoning and justification as being part of mathematics only if this is made explicit. Developing the pupils' ability to take part in the discourse of mathematics enables them to make links and connections across the mathematical system. Pupils begin to see mathematics as a way of explaining, reasoning and justifying, and that the language of mathematics, including non-verbal aspects, has been developed to do this effectively.

Bridges between discourses

Pupils need to make connections, bridges or crossings between their informal discourse and the mathematics register; they are very reluctant to use mathematical vocabulary and phrasing. Lessons using bridging approaches, such as refining the pupils' own attempts to produce a mathematical definition rather than imposing a 'correct' definition, enable pupils to become more adept and more comfortable using mathematical language. Such approaches help the pupils know that they are able to express their own mathematical ideas and are able to use mathematical language. As pupils come to know more vocabulary and are required to express their mathematical concepts more often, they also begin to correct one another in their use of the mathematics register. That is, they begin to make a connection between mathematical language and their own ways of expressing ideas.

It is important to explore the ways the mathematics register fits with, and differs from, the language that pupils use from day to day, otherwise the pupils will be confused and distanced from mathematical ideas. Some pupils find expressing mathematical concepts very difficult and often worry that peers will make fun of them when they try. It is important, therefore, that the classroom ethos recognizes the pupils' difficulties and is supportive and inclusive.

In using mathematical language to explain their ideas, many pupils have to use a discourse that they have not yet made fully their own. It is unsurprising that they feel insecure and open to ridicule when they attempt to act as though they know about mathematics when they do not think of themselves in that way. However, expressing and explaining their ideas helps pupils to learn and to feel that they know them. They take ownership of their ideas and become able to control and use them. This could easily develop into a chicken and egg situation; however, when teachers slowly and carefully nurture pupils' ability to take part in mathematical discourse, they help their pupils to be able to express, and to feel confident about their ability to use, mathematical ideas.

Action research

The main part of this book is about how teachers can act in the classroom to nurture their pupils' ability to use mathematical language so that they can learn effectively. However, first, I will explain why I am so confident that these ideas work and recommend a way of acting that will enable teachers who are seeking to develop their practice to track the changes in their classroom and consider how to make further improvements.

When I started to develop the concepts that this book contains I was a mathematics teacher in an inner-city comprehensive school. The completion of the piece of research (Lee 2004) that underpins the majority of this book led, as it often does, to a change in career that allowed me access to other teachers' classrooms. As they developed practice that reflected my initial ideas I, in turn, learnt more about what it meant to put those ideas into practice. I began to see that the thoughts that had started as an imperative to increase the discourse in my own classroom were powerful in increasing learning because they linked and intertwined with Assessment for Learning. Once the pupils were articulating what they really knew, could do or understand, both I and the pupils could act to increase their learning; I no longer had to guess what would help my pupils – they could tell me. The ideas that started in a small way in my own classroom were tested, proved and extended by many other skilful practitioners that I was lucky enough to work alongside.

I used theory that existed, and that is reviewed in Chapter 6, to attempt to improve my pupils' ability to use mathematical ideas.

> Action research may be defined as *'the study of a social situation with a view to improving the quality of the action within it.'* It aims to feed on practical judgement in concrete situations, and the validity of the 'theories' or hypotheses it generates depends not so much on 'scientific' tests of truth as on their usefulness in helping people to act more intelligently and skilfully.
>
> (Elliott 1991, p. 69, original emphasis)

I knew that I wanted to act more 'intelligently and skilfully' in my classroom and I knew that I had to improve the quality of the learning that was going on. I knew that other authors considered that increasing the discourse in mathematics would increase the learning that pupils were able to do. Now, I thought, how do I increase discourse in my classroom? I tried, and sometimes I failed, and the pupils were confused and irritated by what I asked them to do. But mostly I succeeded a little, and then a little more, as both my pupils and I became more used to what worked and what did not. I found out, by trial and improvement, or, since it was a disciplined study, by action research, how I could support pupils in articulating their own mathematical ideas and I saw that they knew that they learned more this way.

I completed three cycles of action research in order to investigate how I could implement practice that responded better to the ideas that I had acquired through my reading. That is, I planned how to act in the classroom using the theory that I had developed up to that point in time, I implemented those plans and reviewed what I had found out. The implementation and reviewing elements of the action research cycles had three results:

1   a deeper understanding of the various theories that I was reading about
2   a need to search the existing literature to find out more about certain aspects of what I saw happening
3   an expansion or re-articulation of existing theories so that they better reflected the realities of the classroom.

Throughout the three cycles I changed and developed my theoretical perspective. I used my analysis of the data to start to articulate the opportunities and issues of using language in a mathematics classroom and to make this public. The fact that I was a teacher during the data-collection phase of this project was vital to the project and gave strength to its outcomes. I was in a position to create and view the data with a depth of insight given by my intimate involvement in it. My involvement in the 'messy real world of practice' (Griffiths 1990, p. 43) meant that it was difficult at times to collect the data that I needed, but also gave urgency and strength to defining the outcomes. I really wanted to know what my research was indicating as I wanted my practice to be as good as it could be.

The research project

I knew that I wanted to change my practice and I had ideas of how I might go about it; however, I knew that although I would eventually want to use the ideas I was exploring throughout my classes I could not change everything all at once. I picked one class that I got on well with, a Year 9 class (aged 13 and 14 years), with a range of abilities, although none of the pupils felt that they were 'good' at mathematics. I knew that if the ideas worked with this class I could be fairly confident that they would work for most pupils. I also felt that these pupils could achieve much better results in mathematics if I could offer them better learning experiences.

I collected data as I went through the action research cycles. My primary data source was a journal that I kept. I filled in the journal as far as pos-sible after every lesson during the two terms that I researched my practice with this class. In this journal I not only recorded my planning for the class lessons but also detailed thoughts on the pupils' responses to the plans and the way I thought my overall aim of increasing the discourse was progressing. I also used the pupils' notebooks as data and I recorded some lessons so that I could review them later. At the end of the year I conducted informal interviews with groups of pupils where I sought their views about the way that we had interacted within the lessons.

It is hard to collect data when you are teaching; there is so little time. However, I disciplined myself to keep records and I chose ways to record that fitted in with the rest of my work. I made sure that the cycles of the action research fitted in with the terms of the school year, using the breaks for reflection, review and re-planning of the next cycle.

The outcome of the action research cycles

The outcome of the process was for me a surer appreciation of why pupils need to articulate their mathematical ideas, the barriers that prevent them from being able to do so and a series of practices that would enable pupils to develop their ability to express their mathematical thoughts. I also discovered that when pupils started to engage in dialogue in the classroom their learning improved, and both the pupils and I knew what the state of their understanding was and were able to act to increase that understanding.

Action research is a powerful tool to develop teachers' professional practice. The discipline of noticing (Mason 2002) what goes on in a classroom, and reflecting on whether it is as good as it can be, improves the quality of a teacher's own teaching and their ability to share it with others. Action research demands that teachers both think about their own practice and engage with other authors' and colleagues' ideas about what constitutes good practice as they try to improve the quality of their own methods. Action research is a medium through which academic theory can be realized in the classroom.

2 Mathematical language – what it is and what it isn't

Part of learning to talk like a mathematician is to be able to use language both to conjure and control personal mathematical images, as well as to convey them to others.

(Pimm 1995, p. 40)

In this chapter I explore what mathematical language actually is and what pupils will have to learn in order to be able to talk about their mathematical ideas. I discuss the conventional mathematical style and how that can cause barriers to pupils who are learning mathematics, and investigate what ideas it is essential for the pupils to learn in order to express mathematical concepts and to engage with others in mathematical discourse.

Research on mathematical discourse and pupils' reading of mathematical texts concludes that the language in which mathematics is expressed, instead of helping pupils, is actually a barrier to their learning (Pimm 1987; Laborde 1990; Ervynck 1992). The fact is that much of the mathematical discourse that our pupils experience is expressed in a conventional mathematical style. If pupils are to fully engage in mathematical discourse both within and outside the classroom then they must be able to engage with the conventions of mathematics language and teachers must help them to do this.

The way that mathematics is expressed by textbooks, and by many teachers, does not correspond well to pupils' usual linguistic habits. In a classroom it is more usual to hear pupils say, 'You times the length by the width and you get the area' than the passive and more conventionally mathematical, 'The area of a rectangle is equal to the length multiplied by the width.' Although both of these statements express the same concept, the second is conventionally regarded as the more mathematical of the two, as it is expressed in a concise, impersonal and timeless style. There is a complex interaction between linguistic, conceptual and social aspects of pupils' learning (Laborde 1990). Therefore, difficulties posed by the language in which mathematics is expressed adversely affect pupils' conceptualization of mathematical notions.

Pupils become aware of the conventional mathematical style through exposure to mathematical texts and frequently through the way their teachers express mathematics when explaining it to them. Pupils do not develop mathematical means of expression as a matter of course and pupils may consider that they cannot 'do' mathematics because they cannot, or are unwilling to, use the distant, impersonal authoritarian style that they see as recognisably mathematical. Pupils participate in mathematics when they intentionally develop new mathematical ways to organize their experience or reflect on the organization, strategies and concepts that they have already developed. Pupils 'do' mathematics when they develop their own mathematical knowledge and when they use language to express their mathematical ideas and explore their new experiences. It is not necessary to use the conventional mathematical style to do this, but it is important that pupils strive for concision, precision and clarity in their own expressions. Pupils have to focus on expressing themselves with a high degree of exactitude rather than concentrating on striving for richness of meaning, as they may be encouraged to do in their natural language lessons. *'There is no presumption to develop a literature or poetry in MATH [Mathematical language]'* (Ervynck 1992, p. 222). When the way language is used to express mathematical ideas is overtly discussed, pupils can learn to use language to effectively express their thinking.

The mathematics register

Mathematics has a particular way of using language, its own particular way of expressing ideas, which is termed the mathematics register (Pimm 1987, pp. 75–110). The mathematics register is a way of using symbols, specialist vocabulary, precision in expression, grammatical structures, formality and impersonality that results in ways of expression that are recognisably mathematical. The register evolved so that discourse about complex mathematical ideas and processes can take place. A register (Halliday 1975) is not just a collection of words that have been given different meanings or new words developed to express different concepts. It is a way of using language to express concepts and even a characteristic mode of presenting and discussing an argument. The mathematics register is a set of deep-seated linguistic conventions and expectations that have been developed over many centuries and that regulate the way discourse about mathematics takes place. The mathematics register is not static; it is constantly evolving and changing, in part to encompass new ideas that are integrated into mathematical discourse, like discrete mathematics and chaos theory, and in part because of its relationship to natural language which is itself changing and developing.

Registers have, of course, developed in other disciplines; for example, law has specific words that have to be learned to take part in its discourse, such as *tort* and *estopped*, and the same is true for music, science and other disciplines (Pimm 1987; Ervynck 1992, Halliday and Martin 1993, Morgan 1998). Pupils may have to engage in a specific register to be accepted as part of a particular cultural group; rap music, for example, has its own lexis, grammar and ways of expression. Pupils will be aware that there is a different way of expression used in a mathematics classroom than in, say, a history classroom. However, they may not be aware of the depth of the differences and the need to learn to use the register in order to have control over the concepts of mathematics. Registers can also be used as territorial or status markers, as a way to mark some people as being included in a certain group and to exclude others (Gergen 1995). Mistakes in the use of a particular register are often greeted with hilarity by those who 'know'. Again, this is an aspect that pupils may have experienced in their own social life. When teachers focus on developing the pupils' skill in using the register the pupils will feel themselves to be part of a community of people who can use mathematical ideas.

Many aspects that are accepted as part of the mathematics register are the result of convention rather than necessity. Conventional mathematical communication is non-redundant, timeless, non-human and context-independent. Morgan (1999, pp. 58–9) showed that highly respected mathematicians do not always use the conventional style in the papers they write. However, she also showed that most people view a conventional style as more mathematical than other ways of expression, to the extent that pupils were marked higher in GCSE coursework if they used the conventional style to express their ideas than if they expressed the same ideas less conventionally.

The conventional mathematical style has no extraneous words. The style that is conventionally mathematical communicates only what is necessary. There should be no 'extra' or redundant words in the communication. Pythagoras' theorem can be stated: 'In a right triangle the square of the hypotenuse is equal to the sum of the squares on the two adjacent sides.' There are no redundant words in this sentence. However, Pythagoras' theorem could also correctly be stated, 'In a right-angled triangle, if you add together the squares of the length of the two shorter sides then the answer is equal to the square of the length of the hypotenuse.' These extra words may make a sentence more accessible to people learning mathematics but they also introduce human activity or context, which are not considered necessary in the conventional style. People who think the conventional style is important may say that such words show that the writer or speaker is insufficiently knowledgeable to recognize the redundancy of the

LIVERPOOL JOHN MOORES UNIVERSITY
LEARNING SERVICES

information given. In the previous example, the words 'angled' and 'the length of' are redundant as a 'right' triangle is assumed to have a right angle and, in this context, the number associated with the hypotenuse that is to be squared must be its length.

The conventional mathematical style is also an atemporal, concise and impersonal style. The impersonal style is an accepted convention in much academic writing and particularly in mathematics. The use of the passive voice and deletion of personal pronouns is a feature of mathematical discourse and these contribute to the 'distant authorial voice' (Morgan 1995, p. 14) which is common in mathematical texts. A mathematical style is also compact: 'Professional users of [mathematical language] show a constant tendency to keep their language as simple and concise as possible' (Ervynck 1992, p. 222). Mathematical symbolism intends to remove the context of expressions and thereby make them simpler. Rendering the sentence 'The number of pupils in a class, which can be called x, is always greater than the number of teachers in a class (y)' as $x > y$ simplifies the sentence and makes it available for mathematical operations such as linear programming problems. The symbols retain the mathematically important information and the context need only be referred to again when stating a solution. It is also true that many steps are omitted in mathematical discourse, particularly, but not exclusively, in written discourse, in order that the resulting text is as compact or concise as possible. Reading mathematical texts often requires that the reader should regenerate these missing steps. Even something as basic to the language of mathematics as an equal sign can contain hidden meanings. It can mean an equation, as in $(x - 1)^2 = 2x + 3$, or an identity, as in $(x + 1)^2 = x^2 + 2x + 1$, or an equality, as in $f(2) = 5$, where f is a given function. There are others, each implying subtly different concepts. The context of the mathematical situation implies the way that the symbol is to be read.

Important features of the mathematics register

The mathematics register and the conventional mathematical style should not be confused. The conventional mathematical style does make full use of the mathematics register but it is possible to use the mathematics register, that is, to talk and write about mathematical concepts, without using the conventional mathematical style. Pupils can and do use the mathematics register to express their own mathematical ideas and concepts although they may not be using the conventional mathematical style. The demands of the conventional mathematical style could possibly prevent recognition of pupils' understanding of mathematical ideas because they feel unable to articulate their ideas in that style. Therefore, it is important that a teacher overtly acknowledges that even though this particular style often appears in the mathematical texts that pupils encounter, their pupils do not have to use it. Rather they should strive to express their ideas clearly and precisely using appropriate vocabulary and their own ways of expression. Discourse in the classroom should aim for a lack of ambiguity and confident use of essential vocabulary rather than the impersonal, atemporal, non-redundant style that is conventionally mathematical.

It is important to remember that ordinary English is, in general, flexible in terms of how it conveys meaning, and the meaning that makes most immediate sense to the hearer or reader is most likely to be the meaning that is chosen. Flexibility is not an option in mathematics and for that reason symbols are often employed in order to assure precision of expression. Pupils who are starting to express their mathematical ideas in language will not achieve such precision but with support will become more proficient at expressing their mathematical concepts clearly and unambiguously, that is, more proficient at using the mathematics register.

Specific vocabulary

The mathematical register has a specific vocabulary (Otterburn and Nicholson 1976; Shuard and Rothery 1984; Halliday and Martin 1993; Tapson 1997) It uses words in three categories:

1   words that have the same meaning in everyday language as they do in ordinary English – the words that are used to set mathematics in context
2   words that have a meaning only in mathematical language – hypotenuse, isosceles, coefficient, graph, take moments
3   words that have different meanings in mathematical language and natural language – difference, odd, mean, volume, value, integrate.

There are two issues raised by the vocabulary of the mathematics register in helping pupils to learn about mathematics. The first is that even though the words used in a mathematics classroom may be similar to the words used in everyday situations, sometimes there is a need for the pupil to think about them differently in mathematics. This is because the context of a problem is often not intended to be seen as reality in mathematics. For example, if a problem asks about the number of trips a lift must make to transport a number of people to the top floor, it is a reasonable assumption that if it takes a long time, a few people will decide to walk. This is not to be considered when arriving at the answer in a mathematical problem. 'Real world' problems are introduced in order to demonstrate that mathematics is accessible, real and tangible. However, the power of mathematical ideas is that they are abstract and not contextual and it will help pupils if they become aware of this. The second concern is that some words are employed with different meanings even within mathematics – for example, 'square' (a geometric shape and to multiply a number by itself), 'base' (the base of a triangle and base of a logarithm) and 'tangent' (a trigonometric ratio or a line, curve or plane that touches another curve or surface at one point but does not cross it).

Complex syntax

It is often the syntax of the conventional style that causes problems for pupils engaging with mathematics. The conventional presentations of mathematics – deleting personal reference and the consequent use of the passive voice – sometimes make complex syntax inevitable. It is not always necessary to make the syntax complex in the framing of mathematical problems; however, if the writer feels they must use the conventional, impersonal, passive voice then complex syntax is sometimes inevitable.

The following is a quote from an 'A' Level textbook:

> The set of integers is sufficient for many purposes, but we soon need to introduce fractions. Any number that can be expressed in the form a/b where a and b can take any integer value except $b = 0$ is called a *rational number*. All the integers are rational as they can be expressed in the form $a/1$. If we extend our set of integers Z to include all rational numbers, we have the set of rational numbers Q.
>
> (Sadler and Thorning 1987, p. 1)

This quote is from the introduction of the book and is, I would say, maintaining a style that is intended to be readable for the pupils likely to be using it. It uses 'we' and 'our' in several places in order to include the reader in the ideas that it is portraying. It is noticeable that where a definition of the mathematical concept of rational numbers is introduced the passive voice is used, returning again to the inclusive style after the definition. The passive voice is used here in order to make the definition absolutely precise, although the syntax may have been simpler using an active style. For example, 'We define a rational number as any number that we can express as a/b; where a and b are integers and b can take any number except 0.' However, it is clear from this short section that textbooks use the passive voice for introducing mathematical ideas despite the complexity of the syntax.

Sometimes the passive voice has to be used to make a mathematical statement because the active voice would introduce unnecessary complications. A phrase such as 'each side of the equation is divided by three' is difficult to render 'active', as then the personal 'you', or even 'we', would have to be introduced. As I have discussed above, 'you' or 'we' are often introduced in order to make the reader feel included in the text. However, this can itself be confusing to the reader in the case above, as they are unlikely to have been involved in doing the division. As pupils become more familiar users of mathematics, this phrase would not be seen, but rendered $3x = 15 \Rightarrow x = 5$, assuming the division by three. Using the passive voice in mathematics, when pupils are unfamiliar and inexpert users of it in English language lessons, is another barrier to pupils feeling that they are able to read about and use mathematical concepts.

Use of metaphor to convey meaning

Metaphor is involved at every level of mathematical discourse: functions *obey* rules, a function *is a machine* and an equation *is a balance*. These metaphors are useful in the development of mathematics but their presence is not always acknowledged. Indeed just recognizing that a metaphor is being used can be difficult because of the way that the mathematics register is constructed and used. As with the use of metaphor in everyday language, stretching a metaphor too far can result in its failure. The idea that an equation *is a balance* works very well until negative numbers are included in the problems to be solved. If the pupil is relying on that metaphor, and not the underlying mathematical concepts about equations, then they will have no idea how to proceed when the metaphor breaks down. The persistent use of metaphor rather than simile (for example, a function *is* a machine rather than *is like* a machine) has great potential for confusion and misconception as pupils make their way into the mathematics register.

> If pupils are not accustomed to mathematics making sense then having tried and failed to make literal sense of a statement, they are likely to give up as there is nothing to indicate they are grappling with something new.
>
> (Pimm 1987, p. 109)

The naming power of the mathematics register

A word or expression in the mathematics register has the power to evoke a complex web of ideas that make up a mathematical concept. Correct vocabulary is very important because of the naming power of the mathematics register, which is the power of the name to allow the pupil to conjure, use, transform and control mathematical ideas to solve problems. If pupils are asked to employ their own names for mathematical ideas that they develop, they can become more aware of this aspect of the mathematics register and more able to exploit this feature.

Issues in using mathematical language in the classroom

Mathematical language as an additional language

Since the specific way that mathematics is expressed closely resembles a separate language with many of the features of a natural language, it is reasonable to explore whether teaching mathematics as if it were a second foreign language may help pupils overcome some of the barriers to learning presented by using the mathematics register. Learning a foreign language requires pupils to master the words, grammar and syntax of the language and also to be initiated into the culture which uses the language to express certain ideas and concepts. The language of mathematics must be learned in order to be able to express the ideas and concepts that form the academic discipline of mathematics, and by learning the language pupils begin to be enculturated into it.

Learning to 'mean' as a mathematician

The fundamental purpose of any natural language is to serve as the expression of a set of ideas. Mathematics is fundamentally about 'meaning'. Language is used to express mathematical concepts and the interaction between and relationships within these concepts. Each natural language expresses mathematics using words from that language but also uses ways of expression that are recognizable as mathematics throughout the world. It is true that 'fluency in a foreign language is achieved through the ability to think in this language' (Ervynck 1992, p. 219). Therefore, to be fluent in mathematics the pupils must be able to think in mathematical language. It is possible to equate fluency in mathematics with being knowledgeable or having control over mathematical concepts (Pimm 1987; Gergen 1995). In an ideal situation, mathematical language is overtly introduced as mathematical thinking is taught. It is in making use of this mathematics register for their own purposes that pupils come to 'mean' like mathematicians: 'Children need to learn how to mean mathematically, how to use mathematical language to create, control and express their own mathematical meanings as well as to interpret the mathematical language of others' (Pimm 1995, p. 179).

'Doing it right'

Many people express the opinion that there is one correct or right answer to every mathematical problem, and this is probably true for most of the problems that pupils in school will meet. The problem with viewing mathematics as having this degree of certainty is that it dissuades pupils from taking risks. If there is one right answer then all other answers must be wrong and therefore hazarding a different answer may be too big a risk. Pupils often extrapolate from the fact that there is one right answer to a view that there is one right way to pursue a solution to a problem. This way of thinking about mathematics can present a major barrier to pupils discussing their ideas or thinking of different ways to tackle a problem. They would prefer to be given the 'right' way to proceed so that they do not risk appearing stupid by being wrong.

Many pupils worry about 'doing it right', and, when they are unsure, they may prefer to do nothing. What at first sight may appear to be laziness may be the pupils preferring to be 'thought lazy rather than stupid' when they are not sure how to 'do it right'. Teachers have to work very hard to overcome the pupils' deep conviction that there is a single 'right' way to solve a problem and their tendency to want to use that single way, rather than a way that fits better with their own previous experience. Pupils will sometimes opt to copy a poorly understood algorithm rather than improve on a small mistake in their own methods.

Pupils can be persuaded that it is worth offering different ideas provided they feel that their thoughts are valued and respected and that it is safe to take risks in order to improve their understanding, but this will not happen quickly. Peer and self-assessment approaches can help pupils build an idea of all the shades and nuances that amount to a high-quality outcome. Pupils then build a confident knowledge that they are 'doing it right'.

There are other forces at work when pupils express their concern that they are not 'doing it right'. Many pupils have the idea that they have a predetermined level of ability and they are worried that this level is low; this is an 'entity theory of learning' (Dweck 2000). Pupils may have reasons to fear that they have a low level of ability: marking processes that do not explain to the pupil how to improve their learning, teachers who do not use success criteria to show the pupils how well they are learning, and the setting process (grouping by ability) that is common in UK secondary schools. A more effective approach is to assume that everyone can become better able to use mathematical ideas with effort from themselves and help from others that addresses their particular difficulties in learning. This is the incremental theory of learning. If pupils find some work difficult that is 'good' because they can now start learning, and not 'bad' because they have reached the limit of their abilities. It is important to emphasize the incremental view of learning in an environment that uses talk as a tool for learning mathematics and supports everyone in expressing their ideas and uncertainties.

Conclusion

The language of mathematics is distinctive and does use particular vocabulary and ways of expression, called the mathematics register. Some features of the mathematics register are potentially confusing for pupils learning mathematics; for example, words that have two (or more) meanings, the use of metaphor, or the determination that mathematical expression will be as concise as possible. The teacher's role is to mediate between the discourse of mathematics and the discourse that pupils routinely use, to make bridges between the discourses so that the pupils become able to use mathematical language to conjure ideas and to explore and communicate those ideas.

Almost as soon as pupils start formal schooling they will encounter the conventional mathematical style of expression, which is impersonal, atemporal, non-redundant and concise. It is not necessary for the pupils to use this style themselves and many professional mathematicians do not. However, it is desirable that pupils become more proficient in using and reading this conventional style so that they are more able to take part in the wider discourse of mathematics and because they are often assessed as being a better mathematician if they are able to use the conventional style.

It is important that pupils use mathematical language themselves. They will then be able to express their understandings and their misunderstandings so that they are in a position to learn more. They will also be able to transform mathematical concepts into new situations, and take control over their mathematical ideas. Pupils who are able to use mathematical language to express their ideas are able to communicate with one another and their teacher, they are able to both build and share meanings of words and expressions, and ultimately learn mathematics effectively.

3 Starting to talk in the mathematics classroom

In Chapter 2, I set out what constitutes mathematical language and the potential barriers to learning that could be created by language as it is used to express mathematical ideas. In this chapter, I look at ways to interact in the classroom to help pupils to learn to use mathematical language in order to deepen their understanding of mathematics. I deal with issues such as organizing the classroom and ensuring an inclusive ethos, and make practical suggestions for how to achieve a talking and learning classroom. I do not provide ready-made recipes for action but rather principles to guide thoughtful teaching. Teachers often like to 'see what it would look like', and, towards the end of the chapter, I describe several lessons where the principles described are put into action.

Organizing the classroom

The first and most important consideration in setting up a classroom where pupils are going to use talk as a way to learn mathematics is the organization of the classroom. If pupils are to talk and listen to one another then they have to be able to see and hear one another. I know that this seems obvious but it is something that often, in my experience, mathematics teachers do not think about. In a mathematics classroom, there are many problems and barriers presented by the way that language has to be used when expressing mathematical ideas; it is important that the classroom does not set up additional physical barriers. Pupils find articulating mathematical ideas problematic and asking pupils to raise their voices to do so presents a further, unnecessary barrier.

There are many reasons to think about how pupils are positioned within the classroom.

If pupils can hear one another then teachers do not have to repeat or echo what pupils say. Repeating or echoing pupils' communications means that the teacher intervenes in everything that is said. The discourse is not 'owned' by the pupils as it always goes through the teacher and it is almost impossible for pupils to respond to one another as they are always responding to the teacher. Teachers often change what is said by the pupils when they repeat it. The emphasis changes or often the words themselves change, usually to include language that is more mathematical. When the teacher acts in this way pupils themselves do not need to use mathematical language as the teacher will supply the important vocabulary or phrasing. Repeating or echoing what pupils say is counterproductive if the teacher wants pupils to use mathematical language themselves to express and discuss their own ideas.

If pupils can see and hear one another, they can listen to what is said and build up an understanding of mathematical concepts. Pupils and teachers gain much from listening to one another; in fact listening is where Assessment for Learning comes into action. Pupils hear another person's ideas and can judge how far those ideas coincide with their own. They are then in a position to self-assess, and ask themselves questions such as:

- Do I agree with what was said?
- Do I disagree with what was said and/or want to remind the speaker of something they may have forgotten?
- Do I feel unsure about what was said and want to ask a question to clarify the ideas?
- Do I know something that would add to what was said?

By asking themselves these questions, pupils can get immediate feedback on their current understanding. If they ask follow-up questions or make further statements they are both adding to the knowledge being built up in the classroom, and putting themselves in a position to receive immediate feedback from their peers.

When pupils are used to using discourse as a learning tool they do not consciously ask themselves the questions set out above, but they do think in that way. Rather than thinking, 'Do I agree?' or 'Do I have anything to add?', the pupils are concentrating hard on the concept being discussed and on understanding as much about that concept as they possibly can. However, if pupils are finding discussion hard, as they often do in mathematics, then asking them to think about these questions as they listen to one another gives them clear guidelines for how they should respond to one another. Using these questions also makes clear that each individual pupil will extend their own understanding by contributing to the overall discussion – some pupils need this reassurance.

While pupils are listening and responding to one another and considering the ideas put forward, teachers can also listen and observe. If the conversation is developing erroneous ideas teachers can intervene appropriately. If the conversation is stuck, ideas or connections can be offered that can re-start the discussion. If pupils go beyond the teacher's expectations, they can add to their knowledge. When teachers actively listen to their pupils they can know what pupils are actually thinking and understanding and can intervene with appropriate learning activities. Again, this is Assessment for Learning really working to extend the learning in the classroom.

When pupils can see and hear one another the discussion becomes a learning conversation between pupils which can be extended to smaller-group work. When whole-class discussion is conducted in a way that pupils can see and hear one another they will begin to see that this is a good way to learn. Whole-class discussions can serve as a model for conversations during small group work. In my experience, pupils quickly become able to use mathematics language to express their ideas in whole-class discussions, but are slow to do this in small-group work. During whole-class discussions, teachers are able to support and encourage, and indeed demand, that their pupils use mathematical language to express mathematical ideas, but this is not the case in small-group work. However, when pupils use mathematical language in small groups, more of them will have the opportunity to benefit from articulating their thoughts. Discussing ideas together as a whole class will begin to support pupils in using mathematical language in small groups. It is often necessary for pupils to discuss together as a class initially in order to build a mathematical register for themselves that allows them to discuss their mathematical ideas in smaller groups.

So pupils have to be positioned in the classroom so that they can see and hear one another. There are as many ways to do this as there are classrooms, but here are two suggestions:

Ask pupils to move to the front of the classroom and gather around the board. This has always been my favourite way of conducting conversations in my classroom; this is because when pupils are close together:

- they can easily speak to one another; they do not have to raise their voice at all and therefore the conversation is more natural; I have found that even pupils who in other situations may have been reluctant to answer joined in the conversations when they were surrounded by others struggling to understand a mathematical concept
- they can listen and respond to one another; pupils hear one another's ideas easily when close together, and are much more likely to think about what someone is saying and respond to it
- it is hard to opt out – everyone is more naturally involved in the conversation; in a normal classroom situation, it is possible for a teacher to find that someone has not answered any questions or joined in the conversation for many lessons; these are pupils who

do not catch the teacher's eye or seem to 'hide' behind their desks; when gathered close together they are more likely to join in and the teacher can act to make sure that they do, by asking for specific contributions or by asking the group itself to check that everyone has been involved

- the teacher is better able to enforce a classroom ethos; if a pupil 'has a go' but makes a mistake, the teacher can instantly identify and sanction any 'sniggers' or inappropriate behaviour; however, I have found that by gathering pupils together they are much more likely to behave well; it emphasizes that this is a conversation and not a competition – we are working together to improve everyone's understanding and everyone can, and should, ask questions or offer ideas.

Many primary teachers ask pupils to sit together 'on the carpet', away from the distractions of their desks, to concentrate on talking and learning at the start and end of lessons. I would not suggest that secondary school age pupils be asked to sit on the floor, but otherwise the idea is the same: gather the class close together so that they know that this is the time for thinking, talking and learning. It is relatively easy for pupils to stand for the time that is needed, or they can bring chairs or 'perch' on desks. Teachers can act as initiators of the conversation at first, setting out the learning objective and asking questions for the class to consider. They can then go on to act as 'scribe' and record any important points that are developed. Teachers actively listen and observe so that they can intervene as and when it is appropriate, and really come to know what their pupils know, understand and are capable of.

Arrange desks in a U-shape. This arrangement is favoured by many Modern Foreign Language teachers, who also need their pupils to listen and talk to one another. In this organization, pupils can see and hear one another fairly well and they can record ideas that are discussed in their notebooks or on small whiteboards if that is appropriate. Pupils may well have to raise their voices a little when contributing but they quickly become used to this and the teacher can ask for answers from certain areas of the room at different times to ensure that everyone is involved in the discussion. If teachers want their pupils to discuss ideas in small groupings first before contributing to a whole-class discussion this arrangement is ideal. This layout is preferred by teachers who use whole-class discourse extensively in their teaching, as it is quick and straightforward to call the class together to discuss a point that has arisen in individual or group work. Pupils can easily talk to one another as they are able to see most of the class, and the teacher can listen and observe as well.

The organization of the classroom is important if pupils are to learn to use mathematical language themselves. The organization should allow pupils to see and hear one another without the need to raise their voices too much. Pupils will support one another in their learning if they are encouraged to do so by the learning activities they are engaged in and the organization of the discussion.

Including everyone in the discourse – getting the ethos right

Including all pupils all the time in the thinking and the discourse is an impossible dream, but teachers can strive to improve this aspect. Organizing the classroom so that pupils can see and hear one another and the teacher certainly helps with inclusion but there are other ideas that can be tried. The first and most important is to ask questions and set activities that all pupils see as worth thinking about. I will deal with this aspect in a later section in this chapter. The second is to set classroom mores that make clear that the teacher expects everyone to be ready to contribute. The third is for the teacher to make sure that everyone has the opportunity to contribute during a group of lessons.

'No hands up'

When pupils raise their hands to contribute to the discussion they have to wait for the teacher to indicate that it is their turn to speak, all contributions are sanctioned by the teacher, and pupil-to-pupil dialogue is discouraged and is often not possible. Sometimes it is appropriate for the teacher to ask for contributions from pupils but the teacher will want to choose which pupil makes those contributions and therefore whether or not pupils raise their hands is irrelevant. I have heard teachers say, 'I wait until most of the class have raised their hands and then I ask someone who hasn't to check that they are paying attention.' Thus raising hands is used as a classroom management strategy. I have been told that raising hands stops pupils shouting out answers. I have seen too many pupils with their hands up 'blurt' out the answer unasked, because they cannot contain themselves any longer, to be convinced by this argument. I know that once pupils put up their hands, they stop thinking about mathematics and start competing to catch the eye of their teacher. I therefore think that 'no hands up' is a good idea for several reasons:

- pupils have quiet thinking time as a matter of course if they do not have to raise their hands; the teacher is much more likely to leave an appropriate time for thinking if the norm in the classroom is not to raise hands

- pupils can use the full time allowed to think about the problem in question; I have seen teachers ask their pupils to 'put their thumbs up' when they have had enough thinking time; this is not a competitive 'I want to answer', just a small movement so that the teacher knows when to start the discussion
- everyone has time for thinking and so everyone will be ready with an answer, even if that answer is 'I don't know'; therefore, no one can 'opt out' by not raising their hand or 'keeping their head down'; it is important that 'I don't know' is an acceptable answer but that must be interpreted by everyone as 'I need to learn'; the teacher will return to pupil at an appropriate time and check that they have learned more from the discussion
- time is used for thinking and not wasted waiting for an appropriate number of pupils to have raised their hands or for the teacher to ask enough of the volunteers to make sure no one feels left out; a teacher once told me that she saves 10 minutes each lesson by not allowing pupils to put their hands up; part of this saving was that the answers that her pupils gave were much more to the point and appropriate and moved the learning forward quickly
- since everyone has had the chance to be ready with an answer more pupil-to-pupil exchanges can be expected, especially if they are used to thinking in the 'self-assessment way' discussed previously; pupils can and do agree or disagree with one another or seek clarification of ideas without going through the teacher, making for a true thinking and learning discussion; I have seen many such discussions happening in classrooms that use these techniques; pupils discuss and develop ideas between themselves, making connections and bringing in ideas from other areas; teachers are able to observe and think about each individual's learning – in fact, the only time they make a contribution to the discussions is when called upon for 'professional' advice about something that the pupils decide that they do not know.

It's OK to get the answer wrong

Pupils often say that they are frightened to contribute to classroom discussions because they may get the answer wrong and be ridiculed by their peers. These worries should not be dismissed, and it is important that they are tackled head on.

Pupils should understand that teachers want to know what they really think or know, as this is important for them to provide the next appropriate learning experience. If pupils fully understand this then they will also know that teachers are interested in all answers, right or wrong. A 'wrong' answer, perhaps more than the 'right' answer, helps the teacher assess what further learning pupils need. 'Wrong' answers may reveal misconceptions that the teacher needs to address and if one pupil thinks a certain way, it is very likely that others will as well. When the teacher knows what misconceptions pupils have she can plan appropriate learning activities. Teachers can assure their pupils that 'wrong' answers are the interesting answers because they reveal what the teacher needs to know.

If pupils always get all the answers right then the work is probably too easy for them. This is not the way that pupils usually think. In fact, they usually assume that if they get an answer wrong that they cannot 'do' mathematics, rather than realizing that they need to put in more effort or think more widely. Teachers can help dispel this notion by discussing it with their pupils. Using such phrases as 'You're finding that hard? Good, you are starting to learn something new!' can help pupils remember that that getting answers wrong is not a indication of lack of ability but shows that they have to start to make an effort to learn.

An inclusive ethos

Once pupils recognize that it is all right to get the answer wrong then some of the fear of ridicule will be dispelled. However, teachers must also recognize that part of the fear of ridicule is generated by using a language that pupils do not feel is their own. If pupils are to express mathematical ideas clearly then they will need to use mathematical language to some degree. They will feel awkward doing this – I know how awkward I feel when I first start to use French on holiday in France, but I also know that this feeling subsides the more I use French. Pupils will feel that they are using language that only 'educated' mathematicians use, and in doing so are acting as educated mathematicians when they are just struggling to understand mathematics. However, the more they use mathematical language the less ridiculous they will feel and the more they will see themselves as able to use mathematical ideas.

Therefore, part of setting out an inclusive ethos in a mathematics classroom is making sure that there are no inappropriate remarks made as pupils struggle to express their mathematical ideas. But another important part is to help pupils become accustomed to using mathematical language themselves so that they can clearly express their mathematical ideas without feeling that they are using someone else's language.

Gemma

Gemma was very negative about mathematics at the start of the research. She did not find the work particularly hard but seemed to see no point in doing it. Gemma was, along with the other pupils, reluctant to articulate her mathematical ideas. In a lesson on Fibonacci's sequence I asked each pair of pupils to work together to write an explanation of how the sequence worked. Most of the pupils described the sequence in the same way but Gemma and her working partner Nina produced a different version.

'The pupils looked at the sequence and produced their own explanations. I wrote each explanation they gave me on the board just as they dictated.
"1 add 1 is 2, 1 add 2 is 3 and so on to get sequence" (from eight groups).
"You add the number in front to get the next" (from Angie and Colin).
"You add the two numbers in front to get the next one" (from Gemma and Nina).'

When I asked the class to decide which of the explanations written on the board was 'the best' they all voted for Gemma's, and they decided to record this explanation in their notebooks. This was an important incident for Gemma: it helped her know that she could use mathematical language to express her ideas and made her become more willing to do so.

Another factor that was important for Gemma was that I allowed her some choice in what she did. She knew what she was intended to learn but how she went about learning the concepts was to some extent her responsibility. She was more prepared to attempt the work when she was allowed to make individual choices and some of her negativity disappeared. Gemma gained in confidence over the year and produced extended work much more willingly. She produced several well-explained written projects, and became more independent and sought less reassurance. She entered into a dialogue with me and her peers that was more equal, discussing ideas, listening to others and offering opinions.

Time is a big issue in learning

Pupils will not be able to articulate their understanding unless they have had time to think and reflect on their ideas; therefore, time to think should be a normal part of classroom practice. Pupils can be given time to think in several ways: they can be asked to think quietly by themselves for a few seconds; they can be asked to talk to a partner and make some decisions for between 30 seconds and a few minutes, depending on the question; or they can be asked to work on a problem for some time as part of a larger group. One way to give pupils time to think and reflect that is often forgotten by teachers is to give them a challenging task to do that requires a great deal of thought and reflection.

Thinking quietly by themselves for a few seconds is a good idea in a whole-class questioning session. Pupils often consider that they should be able to give a single correct answer to all mathematical problems and that they should be able to do this quickly. This idea is fostered by the way that many whole-class questioning sessions are conducted. Pupils are therefore concerned when the work gets more demanding and they cannot give an answer quickly, and may decide that they cannot 'do' mathematics. Of course, sometimes mathematics teachers do want quick answers from pupils, but this should not be the only type of question used. If pupils expect to have to spend time thinking hard and reflecting during all lessons then they will deal with more challenging aspects of mathematics in the same way.

Sometimes in order to give pupils time to think and reflect it is a good idea to ask them to discuss their ideas with a partner. There are many ways to use 'response partners' or 'study buddies'.

- Pupils can be asked to think quietly and write five words that they associate with a concept. If they then discuss these words with a partner they will be far more confident about adding their contributions to a whole-class mind-map or spider diagram.
- If pupils are reluctant to extend their answers in class, especially where they have been used to one-word answers being the correct way to respond in mathematics, then they can be asked to work with a partner to decide on an answer with a minimum length, for example seven or ten words. Again, rehearsing the answer with one another helps pupils feel confident when asked to make their contribution to the class discussion.
- Pupils can be asked to work with a partner to decide on the wording of an explanation of a mathematical idea. If pupils are asked to write their ideas on a mini whiteboard or a scrap of paper these can be displayed for everyone to consider. Once displayed the explanations are dissociated from their authors and pupils can be asked to consider which is the 'best' or which wording or phrasing expresses the ideas most clearly. This helps pupils towards a fluency with mathematical language.

Pupils will get used to thrashing out their initial ideas with a partner and then be ready to contribute ideas to a whole-class discussion that will help build knowledge for everyone. The above ideas are ways to help pupils understand both the way that they are expected to use response partners and the benefit to their learning that can be obtained.

Pupils need time to assimilate ideas, time to work with mathematical concepts and become familiar with them. It can be hard to judge how much time is required for this. Moving on to another topic before they feel confident that they understand and can use the current ideas will make pupils feel that they are unsuccessful learners. However, spending time working with the same ideas, in the same ways, over and over again is tedious for the pupils and that can also make them feel unsuccessful. An answer to this problem can be a challenging task that requires pupils to develop ideas and concepts over a period of time. The pace of lessons has to be judged carefully. Pupils need time to assimilate ideas but lessons must be purposeful and focused. A challenging problem can ask pupils to focus on an idea for longer than swiftly changing short questions, whilst still allowing pupils to see that they are making progress in learning about mathematics.

Requiring pupils to think and reflect is part of the learning process that is set in motion by requiring them to articulate their mathematical ideas. It is also vital in order to use Assessment for Learning. Without time to reflect, pupils may not engage in the reorganization of their conceptions, which is an important part of the learning process. Without time to think, the responses that pupils give will not be a true reflection of their current understanding and therefore the teacher will not have accurate information to guide subsequent teaching activities.

Building a facility with mathematical language

I have explained that it is important that pupils express their mathematical ideas clearly if they are to improve their mathematical learning. I have also talked about organizing the classroom and setting up a classroom ethos so that they are able to express those ideas. The idea that pupils should be given time and opportunity to think and reflect is generic to any learning environment; however, there are special considerations when encouraging pupils to express their ideas in mathematics due to the complexities of mathematical language.

As I explained in Chapter 2, in mathematics the learners have to learn to express their ideas in mathematical language if they are to share those ideas with others. Without mathematical language pupils engage in a great deal of pointing and a lot of 'this one' and 'that one there', which is not the clarity that mathematics aims for, and often leads pupils to conclude that they do not know how to use a mathematical concept when what they do not know is how to talk about it.

Take, for example, this excerpt from a small group of Year 3 children discussing their ideas with their teacher.

T	Have a look at that.
	Teacher shows a board on which is written
	__ ÷ 5 = __ remainder __
	What's the biggest whole number remainder you will get if you divide a number by 5?
P1	4.
T	Why do you think it's 4?
P1	Because it's the biggest number, umm the one that's … use the whole number that you can get under 5.
T	Right, what would happen then if there was a number bigger than 5 there? What …
P1	It wouldn't be, it wouldn't be dividing by 5, umm dividing by 10.
T	I'm going to change that to a three (changes the 5 on the board to 3) so now if I have a number and divide it by 3 what's the biggest remainder I'm likely to get?
P2	2.
T	Why?
P2	Because if you go on 4s it would be on the 5 times table.
T	If I go on 4 it would be the 5 times table … a bit more …
P2	And … (shakes his head) I don't know.
T	No?
P3	If I go up to 3 it's umm you wouldn't have a remainder.

In order to express their ideas clearly, these pupils need to know some vocabulary, for example 'multiple' and 'factor', but they also need to learn how to express certain mathematical ideas, like 'if the remainder was 5 or more, then 5 would go into it another time'. The teacher does not build on the 'the biggest number' or 'if you go on 4s it would be on the 5 times table', which showed that P2 was talking about the size of the gap between multiples of 5, possibly because there was a video camera pointing at her. Since pupils seemed unable to use certain words and expressions, they appear to the teacher and to themselves not to know some mathematical ideas. When P2 says 'And … I don't know', he is admitting that he does not know how to express his ideas and that may have led him to conclude that he does not know about the concept under discussion. The teacher seems to be concentrating on teaching her pupils mathematical ideas and appears, in this extract, not to think about showing them how to use mathematical language to express their mathematical ideas.

It is important that the teacher teaches both the mathematical ideas and how to talk about the mathematical ideas from the very start of schooling. The literacy of mathematics extends beyond vocabulary and must be taken seriously. 'How can we express this idea so that it is clear to us?' should be a common question in a mathematics classroom.

Troy

Troy was 'one of the lads', happy to chat to classmates but not inclined to talk about his mathematical ideas. When I started to try to increase the amount of discourse that involved pupils in the lessons, I noted, *'Troy needs to be forced to think. When thinking he achieves well.'* He was a pleasant boy but was one of the lower achieving pupils in the class.

About a term later, I taught the pupils about Pythagoras' theorem by asking them to draw and measure several right-angled triangles with squares produced from each side, or *'triangles with squares hanging off them'* as one of the boys in the class expressed it. I asked the class to tabulate their results and to articulate for themselves the relationship between the areas of the squares. I then told them that they had stated Pythagoras' theorem. While they were doing their drawings I specifically used the term 'vertex'. I noted that, *'At the start of the second lesson on Pythagoras' theorem one of the boys, Troy, used the word vertex that I had stressed during the previous lesson. He had picked up on using this word.'* The way that I used the word vertex seems to have enabled Troy to know that it was the appropriate term to use and he was prepared to use it himself in the next lesson. Troy was beginning to use mathematical language for himself.

Later in the same series of lessons, I overheard Troy using a phrase for the equals sign that seemed to mean more to him than the more usual term 'equals'.

Troy said to himself as he worked, 'If you add them two small squares together that is the same as the big square.' As he said this, he wrote $a^2 + b^2 = c^2$, firmly writing the two bars of the equals sign as he said 'is the same as'.

The phrase Troy used as a name for the 'equals' sign seemed to help him to use that mathematical symbol in his mathematics. He was expressing a relationship that enabled him to generalize and transfer his knowledge to many different problems. Troy was making great strides forward. He found, possibly for the first time in several years, that he was able to use mathematical ideas to solve problems. He remembered and used the correct vocabulary and applied Pythagoras' theorem to many different and challenging problems. 'Troy seemed to feel very confident with this work; his work proceeds quickly,' I noted in my research journal.

This was the start of a time when Troy discovered how to find out the information he needed and to apply it to solve mathematical problems. He also began to help other people in the class in subsequent lessons. He had changed from 'a lad' who avoided work to someone who supports others in their work. Troy quickly started to use correct vocabulary. I recorded that 'I had a long conversation with Troy and his friend; they used the correct mathematical names for the shapes we discussed.'

Their ability to use the correct terms for mathematical ideas appeared to be linked to the change in their attitude to completing their work. Troy produced several independent pieces of investigational work during this time; they were expressed in a clear and acceptable way, showed his mathematical ideas and were well organized.

Troy became more confident in mathematics, he came to see himself as someone who could use and control mathematical ideas. He used mathematical terminology correctly and used his own expressions, where he felt that was more helpful to him. He was able to use language in the same way as someone who 'knows' about mathematics.

Practical approaches to use in the classroom

Making a clear explanation of a mathematical idea

Many mathematical ideas are hard for pupils to express but it is very important to try. One of the reasons that mathematics seems so difficult to gain control over is that pupils rarely attempt to fully articulate their ideas.

I will use a lesson on Fibonacci's sequence as an example of how to help pupils express their mathematical ideas. This sequence is often used as part of school mathematics. It can be part of some very interesting lessons, as there are several examples of where the mathematical sequence explains naturally occurring patterns. The sequence of numbers looks like this:

1, 1, 2, 3, 5, 8, 13, 21, ...

After a short inspection of these numbers, most pupils seem to have an intuitive idea of how the sequence carries on, however putting it into words can be more challenging. I asked a class who were just beginning to learn to articulate their mathematical ideas to work in pairs to produce a short sentence that 'explained how Fibonacci's sequence worked'. I suggested that they write their sentence down if they wanted to, so that they were sure of the wording they wanted, but they did not have to write. This is what they came up with:

1 add 1 is 2, 1 add 2 is 3 and so on to get the sequence.
You add the number in front to get the next.
You add the two numbers in front to get the next one.

I wrote each explanation on the board, verbatim, as they told me. The first sentence came from about eight groups of pupils, that is most of the class chose to explain the sequence in a literal way using the numbers that formed the sequence. I then asked the class to consider which description 'best described' Fibonacci's sequence. The pupils told me that they felt that the first explanation was only useful at the very start of the sequence and that they knew that sequences continued infinitely. The second explanation included more generalized detail but it did not really describe how to calculate the next number in the sequence, and the pupils asked, 'What do you add "the number in front" to?' The class thought the third definition above was 'best' because it told them exactly what to do and would work wherever you had got to in the sequence.

The pupils' reactions made me aware that pupils knew some of the conventions of the mathematics register. They were able to tell me that the third description was 'best' because it contained sufficient detail and was generalized. Although the third explanation did not use the mathematics register conventionally, as it used personal terms, it was crossing over from the way that pupils naturally use language to the way that language is used in mathematics.

The pupils were asked to attempt to produce a clear expression of their thoughts, to make their transient thoughts more permanent thereby helping them clarify and remember the mathematical ideas that they were learning about. They were also involved in the whole process – they made their initial decisions, they assessed all the various models that I wrote up on the board for them and they then decided for themselves both which was the best explanation and why.

I have wondered looking at this lesson whether I should have let them write up their own sentences on the board. I can see that this would have meant that it truly was their language being looked at. However, in this instance I had not required the pupils to write their explanation if they did not wish to, so asking them to write on the board would have been inappropriate. I did want the explanations written so that they were available for the second part of the process, so I did the writing. I had to be very disciplined with myself as I wrote their explanations on the board to write exactly as the pupils dictated. The temptation to change, abbreviate or 'correct' the language was strong. It was important that I accepted their language and allowed them to assess their ideas against other models of ways of expression. I could also have introduced a 'mathematician's way of explaining' but that would have been too far outside their own discourse and I felt would have reinforced any feeling they had that they could not 'do maths'. Assessing the best from a selection given by their peers gave the pupils models that they could see it was possible to aspire to, reinforcing a belief that they could use mathematical language with a bit of extra effort.

At the end of this session, they reworded their own explanations and wrote down their own articulation of Fibonacci's sequence. The more generalized way of expression – that is, the more 'mathematical' way – had become the way that they used for their own explanation – at least for this lesson!

Correcting someone else's mathematical writing

Asking the pupils to read and correct or mark other pupils' mathematical writing has many of the benefits of the idea described above. Again, this is best described using a lesson, this time on Pythagoras' theorem. By now the class had done quite a lot of work on it and had become confident solvers of problems using the theorem, and I asked them, for homework, to write a description of Pythagoras' theorem and how to use it. At the start of the next lesson I took in all the books and gave them out to other people explaining that they were going to read someone else's description and that they needed to check the work and help each other improve their writing, if necessary. I first gave the pupils time to read the description they had been given. I asked them to think about a good description of Pythagoras' theorem and what it would look like and gave them a minute to do this. The pupils then told me their ideas about what a really good description would contain:

> A diagram showing the squares on the sides of the triangle.
> Pythagoras' theorem using a's, b's and c's the same as on the diagram.
> Some words describing what you could use Pythagoras' theorem to do.
> Some words describing how Pythagoras' theorem worked and what you need to watch out for.
> Two or three different problems using Pythagoras to find the answer.

As you can see, the class were very demanding about what would make up a good description. I asked the class to use these criteria to peer-assess the descriptions in front of them. I asked them to spend some time considering which of the criteria was done well and to explain to their peer why it had been met well. Once this was completed, I asked them to consider one way that their peer might usefully make improvements and to explain how to do this. The pupils did this thoughtfully and well; they were taking on the role of teacher for their peer and they took this work seriously. The work was then returned and the pupils began to work on a second draft of their descriptions. The second drafts were much improved from the first but each was still individual. They did not copy what they had read or seen but rather used the ideas that had been discussed or reviewed to produce their own high-quality work. Those pupils who had already produced a good-quality description made their expressions clearer and devised more challenging examples to show the theorem at work.

I did consider whether the pupils should have had the criteria before they were asked to complete their initial descriptions. I think that most of the time pupils should have the assessment criteria first, but, in this instance, I wanted to gather the criteria from the class, a process that they were not used to at this stage. Therefore, it seemed important that they had put some thought into how to describe the mathematical ideas involved in Pythagoras' theorem before deciding on the criteria for a very good description. I made sure that they had time to use the insights they had gained from the peer-assessment exercise to improve their own work so that they had a very clear articulation of Pythagoras' theorem using their own words.

The link between assessment for learning and learning to articulate mathematical ideas is clear here. The exercise allows the teacher and the pupils themselves to know how broad their understanding of a concept is and whether there are any gaps in that understanding. But that knowledge is available for public scrutiny only if the pupils are able to fully articulate their understanding, and they will need help to do this well. I, as teacher observing the whole exercise take place, came to know a great deal about both the pupils' understanding of Pythagoras and the way that they felt it appropriate to describe their understanding. I was able to use those observations to plan further lessons and further discussions about how to use language to articulate mathematical ideas.

Knowing what words to use and using those words

In most areas of mathematics, it is important to learn both vocabulary and the way that vocabulary is used. Pupils need to use this language themselves in order to get used to the way that the expressions are used and to begin to use the mathematical terms to express the web of concepts and ideas that are encompassed by those terms. In practice, this means that pupils need to say the words aloud and there are many ways to achieve this. I found a way to get pupils started doing this was to use 'old fashioned' chanting. For example, in a lesson on squares and square roots, I asked the pupils to gather close together by the board where I had written the phrases and to chant the unfamiliar words with me. The lesson went as follows:

> We all chanted what I had written on the board: 'If 3 squared is 9 this implies that the square root of 9 is 3.'
> We then chanted, 'If 7 squared is 49 then the square root of 49 is 7.'
> 'What does square root mean?' I asked.

'You times by itself to get the ...' someone hazarded.
'What do you times by itself?' I asked
'The number'.
'What number?' I asked, which resulted in puzzled looks all round.
I reminded them of the definition we were looking for.
'You times the square root by itself to get the original.'
'So what is a square root?'
'It's a number you can times by itself to get the original number,'
several people said together, and I wrote that on the board.

I encouraged the pupils to 'use the mathematics register' in two ways
in this lesson. I required them to:

1   vocalize the words, something that is often not easy for them
2   think about the words and phrases that are used to express these
     mathematical ideas.

Some of the individual pupils struggled to use the words but they succeeded
as a group to create a complete, mathematically correct, definition of a
square root. I asked the pupils to chant the words and ways of expression
so that they all actually vocalized them, but I did not leave it there. I asked
them to think about the words and to transform the words to produce an
inverse definition. I was happy at the time that some of the pupils succeeded in producing a definition of a square root as all of them had been
part of the struggle to support one another in producing the definition.
However, I knew that I could not leave it there and continued to ask individuals to use the words that we had learned together so that I could assess
how much they had learnt and act accordingly.

Sometimes pupils have met the words and ways of expressing ideas
before, but they are still reluctant to use them. As long as they do not use
the words themselves there is no way for teacher or pupils to be sure that
they fully understand the concepts indicated by those words. Sometimes
overcoming these barriers can be achieved by using something as simple as
a 'brainstorm'. The idea is to encourage pupils to suggest the words themselves so that it is possible to assess whether they do know the words and
concepts associated with the objectives for the lessons, and where to begin
with the teaching activities to build on their existing knowledge.

As an example, I started a topic on percentages by asking the class to
write four or five words that they thought were associated with percentages
in their exercise books. I did this in order to give the pupils time to reflect
on their previous experience and articulate what they could remember. One
or two pupils did not write anything. I recorded: 'Most managed one or two
but some could not get started. They didn't know what I wanted.'

I had not explained exactly what I wanted the pupils to write, although I had explained that I wanted to know what they could remember. I felt that the reason that some pupils had not written anything was that they were being asked to write mathematical words, that is, words that were not in their normal social discourse, and therefore they felt unsure about what was required. All the pupils had time to think about their ideas on percentages even if they did not write down any words.

I gathered the pupils together at the front of the classroom and asked them to say what they had written in their books. I wrote all their contributions on the board in exactly the same way as the pupils said them, without rewording. When they realized that all their ideas were acceptable, there were no right or wrong answers, they were far more willing to participate. I recorded:

> *Taking their suggestions, I made an effort to include people who sometimes don't answer. There was a better atmosphere now. Perhaps they were beginning to trust me to accept what they said and themselves to say something sensible. The brainstorming and accepting their ideas, what they said, was important here. I think I might be saying – 'you can talk like a mathematician when you use what you say normally'. Accepting their language, not correcting it, then trying to move forward with it.*

After the 'brainstorm' activity, we completed a table of equivalent fractions, decimals and percentages, the pupils using mathematical language to build their knowledge on the connections between these concepts. I did not have to teach them the connection between the decimal and the percentage; they developed an appreciation of the connection in their discourse. The lesson was successful in including all pupils in discourse that developed meaning because they could see and hear one another and because all the words and phrases came from them. I made it clear that I was not looking for correct answers but rather finding out what the pupils knew and what they did not know, enabling me to start developing further knowledge based on their current knowledge.

Ask pupils to engage with texts

Pupils will meet the conventional mathematical style if they read any published mathematical text, and they do know the type of text that is recognizably mathematical. By secondary school age (age 11 years onwards), pupils can use their experience to judge which ways of expression sound more 'mathematical' than others. The conventional style has been developed in order to clearly and concisely express mathematical ideas.

Therefore, if we are to improve pupils' ability to express their own ideas they need to engage with the conventional mathematical style.

I wanted the pupils to know that the way some textbooks are written may be difficult to interpret, but, with a little work, they are not impossible. One way I found to do this was to distribute several different textbooks that were gathering dust in the cupboard and ask groups of pupils to research the properties of several quadrilateral shapes. I assigned one quadrilateral shape – kite, trapezium, etc. – to each group and told them to find out as much as they could about that shape from the books. They could have just used one textbook but each book gave subtly different information so I suggested that they read all of them and then pool the ideas that they had found. I was very open about the fact that they might find the research difficult and that I did not want them to copy from the textbooks. I suggested that they discuss carefully each property of their quadrilateral they came across, to be able to express it so that the rest of the class could understand.

Each group then had to draft a poster with all the ideas that they had found out about their shape on it. The posters were displayed and all the class looked carefully at each. In front of each poster was a sheet of paper. I asked the pupils to note on this piece of paper any ideas that particularly impressed them on the poster and any questions that they had about a shape that they did not think the poster answered. The posters were then returned to the groups, who continued to work on them to find the answers to the questions that had been written on their sheet. At the start of the following lesson, I asked the pupils to think about similarities and differences between the quadrilaterals that they were investigating. I asked for suggestions of properties of a quadrilateral that they had written about from one group and then asked whether another group had found the same properties or different ones for their quadrilateral. I went round the class asking the same question. If the group did not know, for example, whether the diagonals of their shape crossed at right angles or not, they made a note to find out. I then made a new group to collate the similarities and differences and display these as a poster. The class finished their research and posters, and I used the similarities and differences poster as a stimulus for the plenary discussion, in which I asked questions designed to check the pupils' understanding of the language and concepts associated with quadrilaterals.

In using this approach, I had asked the pupils to engage with the conventional mathematical style and to interpret the ideas that they found in textbooks for an audience of their peers. They were motivated to read the language used in the books carefully and express the ideas themselves. They were also in a supportive environment: if one pupil could not think what a particular phrase meant then others in the group may well have been able to help, and often the process of asking someone else helped the pupil with their articulation. The whole group was further supported in making sure that they had not missed anything, both by seeing what others had unearthed about their quadrilaterals and by being asked questions by other pupils, and by taking part in a whole-class discussion about the similarities and differences in what had been discovered. Both these approaches supported pupils without taking away their ownership of what they produced. They could be confident that they had explained all the properties of their quadrilateral and that they had explained them well, but the language that they chose to use and the way that they chose to display the ideas was a product of their own discussions in their groups. They did the research; they engaged with conventional mathematical language and produced a high-quality product as a result.

Have pupils invent names for mathematical concepts

Mathematical language is used to name concepts and webs of ideas so that these can be discussed and used as models that provide solutions to problems. Mathematics is a system that provides order, and therefore it is important that people use the same names for the same ideas and concepts. However, sometimes in becoming skilled at using the vocabulary and phrasing that is necessary to express the mathematics that they are learning, pupils may lose sight of the fact that someone named those concepts and worked out each particular way of expression at some time. Someone, often a long time ago, had found an obvious connection between the name that was given to a concept and ordinary everyday discourse. I found that helping pupils understand that there was such a connection made the use of the mathematics register less daunting for them.

One approach I used to help the pupils know that there is a connection between the mathematics register and ordinary discourse was to ask them to look at a pattern of dots that formed into squares. The pattern extended like this:

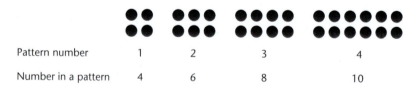

Pattern number	1	2	3	4
Number in a pattern	4	6	8	10

The pupils easily grasped the ideas of extending the pattern of squares by adding two dots to get another square in the pattern of dots and the next number in the number sequence. The class decided that the name of the pattern should be the '2-wide rectangle numbers'. I then moved on to a similar pattern that used triangles as its basic shape and we named the number pattern that resulted ('2-wide triangles' this time). I then asked the pupils to work in pairs to devise their own extending patterns and use them to write down corresponding number sequences. They decided on the names to give their sequences of numbers. My approach of involving the whole class in decisions about what to do next seems to have enabled most of them to know how to go about their task.

I was pleased to see some innovative and well-explained work from these lessons. For example, Philip produced P numbers, which were 6, 11, 16, 21, and so on, which represented the number of dots that he used to make Ps of consecutive sizes. Angie produced Propeller numbers, which were 1, 5, 9, 13, and so on, and she also wrote that 'Propeller numbers go up 4x and go down 3. This is $4n-3$.'

Llewellyn produced a Brochi Number pattern. He wrote, 'My number sequence can be worked out by adding one square on each line. These could be called Brochi Numbers. The algebra is $(n+1)(n+3)$.'

Size of Brochi	1	2	3	4	5
Brochi Number	8	15	24	35	48

Being able to name a mathematical concept enables pupils to evoke that concept, and control and use it to solve mathematical problems. For example, in a percentages lesson the pupils could not remember how to work out 34 per cent of £72 until I reminded them of the term 'decimal equivalent' that we had used the previous lesson:

> I asked, 'How do you work out 34 per cent of £72?'
> They muttered a bit but would not answer, but when I said, 'Do you remember decimal equivalents?' 5 people were now willing to give the answer and one of them said, 'You multiply 0.34 by 72.'

Therefore there are two reasons why helping pupils understand that names in the mathematical register are useful human inventions:

1   pupils can see themselves as mathematicians adding their ideas and names to mathematical discourse just as others have done before them
2   the name of a concept is very powerful in evoking the web of ideas encompassing a concept and enabling it to be used.

Conclusion

In this chapter I have talked about the necessity of organizing the classroom so that everyone can see and hear one another, about the ethos in a classroom where talking about mathematics is the preferred tool for learning, and about practical ideas to begin to build pupils' facility with using mathematical language. Talking is vital in a learning classroom; the majority of people use talk as a way to think through problems and to work out the way forward. The particular way that mathematics is communicated can cause a barrier to pupils' learning because they need to learn how to express mathematical ideas before they can use talk to aid their mathematical learning. In the struggle to learn about mathematical concepts, learning how to talk about those concepts can be forgotten. Learning to talk about mathematical ideas is not just a question of learning vocabulary, although actually using mathematical words is a large part of expressing mathematical ideas. Pupils also need to use ways of expression that are specifically mathematical; they have to learn to be concise, to express the general case rather than the particular. They need to look for the pattern or the system in what they are studying and to use symbols rather than words. The mathematical way of expression, or mathematics register, does not combine well with pupils' natural discourse and therefore pupils have to learn how to specifically express their mathematical ideas in language. When mathematics teachers help them to do this pupils' learning is markedly enhanced.

One of the most important reasons that pupils learn to express their mathematical ideas is that unless mathematics teachers can uncover high-quality information about what their pupils know and understand they will not be able to use Assessment for Learning. The next chapter takes Assessment for Learning as its focus and discusses how pupils who can talk about their mathematical ideas will be able to use Assessment for Learning ideas to reach new and higher standards.

4 Assessment for Learning

Introduction

Assessment for Learning is a way of shaping learning using evidence of pupils' understanding. The better the quality of the evidence about what pupils understand or know or can do, the more accurately the learning activity can be modified to move their learning forward. Pupils can reveal a great deal about their understandings or misconceptions during dialogue in the classroom, but the information that is uncovered will only be of sufficiently high quality if:

- they engage in activities or answer questions that fully explore their understanding
- they have the time both to think through what they know, understand and can do, and to fully express their thoughts
- they are able to use mathematical language to communicate effectively what they know, understand or can do.

Pupils' learning will be enhanced when the information that is uncovered is used to change subsequent learning activity. For example, Assessment for Learning is working in mathematics when:

- pupils explore a problem and find that they can use a mathematical concept easily and then go on to find a more challenging problem to further explore their understanding
- pupils mark a test together in groups and use the results to set out the work that they will have to complete in the next lessons in order to continue to improve their understanding
- teachers use plenaries to explore pupils' understanding of a particular topic by asking searching questions and giving pupils time to think of the answers; they use the knowledge uncovered to plan the next module of work

- teachers observe their pupils as they engage in an activity and see that many of them cannot fully use a particular concept; they use the pupils who can understand to help extend the others' ability to use that concept.

The important facet of each of these examples is that the pupils have the opportunity to express what they can do and what they cannot. When pupils express their understanding the teacher and pupils themselves can be sure of what they understand. Pupils will need to be able to use mathematical language to express their ideas and the time to think about how to articulate them if Assessment for Learning is to be used effectively.

The focus in this chapter will be on Assessment for Learning, but I will assume that pupils will be developing an ability to use mathematical discourse alongside increased Assessment for Learning opportunities in the classroom. I have divided my discussion of Assessment for Learning into four sections: learning objectives and success criteria; questions and answers; feedback; and peer and self-assessment. Each section is not mutually exclusive, each depends upon the others, but for ease of explanation I have focused on each area independently. I discuss how pupils' facility with mathematical language contributes to effective use of Assessment for Learning in each area and how each Assessment for Learning idea contributes to developing the pupils' facility with mathematical language. Assessment for Learning demands that pupils are able to make their thinking public.

Learning objectives and success criteria

Setting out the intended learning for every lesson means that the pupils will understand what they are to learn and both the teacher and pupil can assess progress in that learning. Every lesson should have clear learning objectives and success criteria planned in advance and shared with the pupils during the lesson.

Learning objectives

There are many ways of referring to a basic statement of the intended learning: aim, objective, learning objective, learning intention. Given the choice I would always use 'learning intention' because of the implied flexibility; this is what it is intended we learn this lesson, not what must or even could be learned. However, in England the National Strategy has opted for the term 'learning objective' and therefore it seems sensible to use that term. The National Numeracy Strategy in England has set out clear teaching objectives for mathematics up to age 14. Teaching objectives must be translated into learning objectives for a given lesson. Learning objectives take into account the curriculum objectives set out by the National Curriculum, exam syllabi or by the teacher's own ambitions for the pupils' learning. They also take the pupils into account – their prior knowledge, their speed of learning and the differences within the class. Teaching objectives are often set out in a scheme of work but learning objectives are always specific for a given lesson with a given class.

There are a number of requirements for a learning objective. The learning objective must:

- be planned in advance but flexible enough to take account of pupils' learning within the lesson
- be shared with pupils, and therefore it is sensible that it is planned from the outset in language appropriate for pupils to understand
- be frequently discussed during the lesson and therefore may contain specific language that pupils will learn to use during the lesson
- be about what the pupils are going learn – not what they are going to do
- be about the learning that is to be done not the context in which it is to be learned
- help the pupils understand the connections between lessons or between parts of the lesson.

There are further ideas that must be considered when setting out learning objectives. For example a learning objective may be:

- a short phrase or one or two sentences
- the 'big picture', or quite specific, depending on the particular lesson and where it sits within a series of lessons
- conceivably be a 'big' question that pupils will learn how to answer
- specific about a skill or concept that is to be learned or about the application of those skills.

Learning objectives will for the most part be quite short. Many teachers choose to record them on their 'smart' board, a whiteboard or on a flip chart, and ask the pupils to write them in their books, but none of that is essential. It is important that learning objectives are shared with pupils and that they are discussed at the start, during and at the end of the lesson, and that pupils can refer to them during the lesson. Where literacy is not a problem many teachers find it helpful to write the learning objective where their pupils can see it, then they can assess their progress against it during the lesson.

Success criteria

Success criteria help pupils to see their progress against the learning objective. The learning objective will often be generic; success criteria will always be specific to the lesson. The National Strategy uses the term 'learning outcomes' but teachers tell me that they find this too similar to learning objective and it is difficult for pupils to understand. The term 'success criteria' is explained in Shirley Clarke's work (Clarke 2005) and seems a useful term to use; however, teachers use many different ways of expressing the same ideas, for example, 'method to ...' or 'what we have to do'. Essentially, 'success criteria' are a list, written for the pupils or by the pupils, of the process that they have to go through to succeed in learning the objective. Success criteria are shared with the pupils and discussed so that they fully understand them.

Success criteria should be planned in advance as this sharply focuses the lesson. If teachers know what they intend their pupils to learn, and know how they will demonstrate that they have successfully completed this learning, then the learning activity in the lesson becomes obvious. While at first this seems to be extra work, planning the success criteria plans the lesson and soon reduces the workload.

Success criteria should:

- be planned in advance
- be shared with pupils and therefore be in language appropriate for pupils
- set out the process through which pupils will successfully achieve the learning objective, including learning specific terms and phrases
- be fully understood and used by pupils (often the pupils will be part of setting up the success criteria).

Pupils should have ownership of the success criteria and articulate the criteria for themselves. Where possible the criteria can be gleaned from the pupils; this emphasizes that the success criteria are there for the pupils. Success criteria allow pupils to guide and monitor their progress through the learning so that they know what they have successfully learned and can seek help if they have any difficulties.

Learning objectives and success criteria must enable pupils to understand the learning that they are aiming to do and the progress they are making with that learning. Here are some examples of ways that teachers use to do this.

Using learning objectives and success criteria

Learning objective	Success criteria
To learn about Pythagoras' theorem	I know what 'right-angled triangle' means
	I have:
	carefully drawn 3 different right-angled triangles
	drawn a square against each side, making sure each angle is a right angle
	found the area of each of the 3 squares and put them in a table
	asked one other person for the areas of their squares and put those in my table
	found a relationship between the areas of the squares and stated it using algebra.
To learn more about the uses of Pythagoras' theorem	I know what square root means
	I can:
	state Pythagoras' theorem and know which sides of the triangle the letters refer to
	use it to calculate the hypotenuse of 5 different right-angled triangles with different orientations
	use it to find a short side of 5 different triangles
	use it to find the height of 2 isosceles triangles.

You will notice that the above learning objectives on their own are quite generic – to learn about Pythagoras' theorem, to learn more about Pythagoras' theorem. However, such learning objectives do their job. At the end of the lesson a pupil can ask:

'Have I learned about Pythagoras' theorem?'
They might answer themselves, referring to the success criteria: 'I know that it is about squares hanging off the sides of a right-angled triangle and I know that the two little squares add up to the big one.'

or

'Do I know more about how to use Pythagoras' theorem?'
'Yes, I can find the length of the hypotenuse of any right-angled triangle I make up and I can find the length of the short sides as well. Now what is all this about isosceles triangles?'

More examples of ways to use success criteria

Learning objective	Context	Success criteria – steps to success
Calculate simple percentages and use percentages to compare simple proportions	Mental calculation strategies to support efficient use of a calculator	I can: use mental methods to calculate simple percentages use my existing knowledge and apply it e.g. If 10 per cent of £40 is £4, I can use this to find 15 per cent (half of 10 per cent is 5 per cent, 10 per cent + 5 per cent = 15 per cent), 25 per cent (5×10 per cent = 50 per cent, then half of this)
Recognize the equivalence of percentages, fractions and decimals		I can: convert a percentage to a decimal to aid a calculation e.g. 12 per cent of 45 $= 0.12 \times 45$ or convert a percentage to a fraction to aid a calculation e.g 12 per cent of 45 $= \frac{12}{100} \times 45$
Compare two simple distributions using the range and one of the mode, median or mean	Handling data 3 KS3 question (6–8 2005, P1) see below	I know the meaning of median, mode, mean and range I can explain and give reasons why two distributions differ, with reference to m,m,m and/or range e.g. Two distributions have the same range but one has a median of 6 and the second a mode of 6 I can provide valid interpretations of the data

Big Question
There are 100 values in the set
The median is 90
The mean is 95
I increase the highest value in the data set by 200
Now what are the median and the mean of the data set?

Another teacher wrote the learning objective on the board and sketched pictures of the various steps that the pupils would take as the class discussed and explored the objective. Each pictorial 'success criteria' was ticked off as the class became sure that they had completed that criterion.

However it is done, the combination of learning objectives and success criteria is powerful in enabling pupils to know and to be able to articulate:

- what they are learning
- how lessons connect with each other
- how they are progressing with the learning
- any difficulties that they might come up against
- where they need to concentrate their efforts in order to extend their learning.

Learning objectives and success criteria enable pupils to articulate their progress in learning and teachers to plan suitable teaching activities to extend that learning further. They support pupils in knowing *what* they are learning, *how well* they are learning and *that* they are learning and therefore are important in helping the pupils know that they are successful learners.

Questions and answers

Rich questions are important in implementing Assessment for Learning, they stimulate pupils' thinking, help them build knowledge and encourage them to articulate what they know. The traditional mathematics textbook has been full of 'graduated exercises' where pupils are invited to complete sometimes 10, more often 20 or 30, similar questions, getting slightly more difficult towards the end. The pupils generally enjoy completing these exercises. The questions require little thought; once the initial algorithm is mastered the pupil 'turns the handle and out pops the answer'. The exercise gives a false feeling of success; the pupil completes many questions and gets them all correct, their book contains a great many ticks and that makes everyone feel good. Unfortunately, pupils are usually using an algorithm mechanically without truly understanding what it is or what it is used for. When a problem is encountered that does not fit the pattern of the graduated exercise the pupil does not know how to use the concept, as they cannot use or control it.

At one time I called those questions that made pupils think and transform their ideas about a concept (often the questions at end of the exercise) 'trick questions'. Now I would seek such questions out and use them after an initial explanation of the concept. I would ask the pupils to explore such 'hard questions' together and if they got through only two or three questions in a lesson, provided those questions had made everyone think and talk about the concept and the web of ideas surrounding that concept, I would consider that it was a good lesson.

I had the privilege of watching a lesson where the teacher asked one planned question and the discussion on that question lasted nearly an

LIVERPOOL JOHN MOORES UNIVERSITY
LEARNING SERVICES

hour. During that time the class explored and learnt many things about the way that the angles of a triangle work together and the relationship between the lengths of the sides of triangles. At one point this Year 7 class (aged 11–12 years) considered ideas that older pupils would call the cosine ratio. I could not see one disengaged pupil or one pupil that was not learning. Every pupil seemed to enjoy the lesson and knew that they had successfully learnt more about the geometry of triangles. They also knew that they had engaged with challenging ideas and successfully mastered them. This was a true feeling of success. What was the question? The teacher showed an acute angle which she said was part of a triangle, then asked whether the triangle was scalene, isosceles, equilateral or right angled. It is not only the question you ask, but whether pupils are encouraged to explore ideas, look at the question another way, question one another and articulate their thoughts and ideas. The question could have been answered quickly or explored at length; the teacher's actions within the questioning session made the difference.

Asking questions that are capable of being explored, and then encouraging pupils to think and explore them is an important part of Assessment for Learning. When the right question is asked much information about pupils' understanding or misunderstanding of a concept can be uncovered and appropriate subsequent learning experiences become obvious to both teacher and pupil. Helping pupils to use the particular language needed to express mathematical ideas will make sure that their understanding of mathematical ideas is not masked by their inability to communicate their thoughts.

Devising suitable questions to help pupils learn mathematics can be problematic. Obviously the language that is used to ask a question must be clear and at an appropriate level for the class in question, and must encourage the use of appropriate mathematical language. In brief, useful questions should:

- explore the full range of the learning objective
- be challenging
- cause deep thinking
- provoke discussion
- make connections between areas of mathematics
- build
  - on previous learning
  - on ideas generated in the class
  - towards the learning objective
- provide a window into pupils' thinking
- explore and expose common everyday ideas and misconceptions.

Getting the climate right

The climate in the classroom has to be right if the pupils are going to respond to the challenge, do the thinking and articulate their ideas. I have explored in Chapter 3 many of the practicalities of establishing a classroom ethos that encourages pupils to articulate their thoughts in answer to questions. Here I will expand on a few more points that are important in helping pupils to think and answer the questions that will help them to learn mathematics.

Supporting one another to develop a common understanding is encouraged. Any feeling of competition to be the first to give a right answer involves one success and most people failing. This is not the right ethos to encourage everyone to think and contribute to the discussion. If the question is challenging and requires a great deal of thought then the teacher will want the pupils to try out ideas that might work, but equally might not. The pupils will need to take a risk when answering; they must know that their contribution will be valued as an important step on the road to understanding. Pupils will also need to listen to one another and think about others' contributions. All these ideas are fostered by a supportive atmosphere and destroyed in a competitive one.

Both teachers and pupils must not be afraid to explore wrong answers. The atmosphere in the classroom must value and explore all answers for their contribution to a common understanding. Right or wrong, they can help to build knowledge. If one person is thinking along certain lines then there will probably be others thinking in the same way; therefore, it is important to explore all answers and assess how they may help reach a solution to the problem in hand.

The teacher emphasizes that they are looking for explanations and ideas. The teacher is not looking for 'right' answers but for explanations of the process and ideas that might help. A questioning session helps pupils learn insofar as it encourages them to think at length and deeply. The more pupils continue to explore the concepts and issues within the question, the more they will use and take control over mathematical ideas – the more they will learn. Thinking will be fostered by teachers following up answers, whether they are 'right' or 'wrong', with a question such as 'Why do you think that?' and 'Does anyone have any further ideas about that?' so that all answers are thoroughly explored. In mathematics it is possible to give the 'right' answer for the 'wrong' reason and the 'wrong' answer for the 'right' reason. If all answers are explored it is possible to make sure that neither of these pitfalls prevents the pupils from successfully learning mathematics.

Mathematical learning will be enhanced by discussion about links between what are often compartmentalized chunks of knowledge. Teachers often talk about teaching multiplication or quadrilaterals or expansion of brackets, and rarely think about teaching mathematics. Mathematics is a systematic seeking of patterns that can be used to concisely model the world. Algebra is a good example; the letters that pupils can find so confusing are often discussed as entities in themselves rather than as symbols that model the patterns of behaviour of quantities. If pupils are used to thinking and talking about the links between different topics in mathematics, what is similar and what is distinctive about a certain area, then they will be learning to use the system that is mathematics.

Wait time is essential. If pupils are to respond to a question with more than a simple answer, they must be given time to think. If pupils are to respond with what they really think, know or remember they will need 3 to 5 seconds wait time in whole-class questioning or 30 seconds to one minute if the pupils are to talk to a partner. Many people prefer to call 'wait time' 'thinking time' because it is time set aside for thinking.

Lessons are focused on pupils' learning, not getting through the content at any cost. When teachers first start thinking about using questioning to really explore pupils' understanding they are often concerned that they will not get through the content. In England there is a Numeracy Framework that teachers are advised to use which prescribes the content and the number of lessons for each topic from the National Curriculum. Assessment for Learning demands that pupils spend as much time on a learning objective as they need to successfully learn that objective. Pupils begin to learn effective ways to come to understand mathematics and they get better at learning and, therefore, learn more in a shorter time. Teachers using Assessment for Learning have told me that even if they have to spend longer than planned on one topic, they will make the time up somewhere else.

Pupils will need to spend time becoming accustomed to being asked questions that require more than a simple answer, to thinking about and exploring concepts in mathematics. It is important to be prepared to feel that the class is learning more slowly to begin with. The class will be learning mathematics slowly but they will learn more effective learning skills. Coverage without understanding is pointless and may even be harmful, as pupils will learn that they cannot be successful at learning mathematics.

No hands up – everyone should be ready with an answer. If the classroom is to be a thinking, talking and learning community, the teacher will want to generate an atmosphere where everybody is willing to volunteer their opinion on the problem in hand and where everyone's contribution is valued. Therefore, volunteering an answer is usually unnecessary as the teacher will want to choose who starts off the conversation, and manage the contributions to ensure that all points of view are heard.

It is not easy to start to use 'no hands up' when pupils are so used to putting their hands up. Teachers sometimes ask pupils to sit on their hands and release the hands at the end of the 'thinking time'. Once discussion is properly established the natural rules of conversation take over and pupils take their turn as adults do in conversation. However, it is useful to begin with to remind them that the rules have changed in mathematics. Another useful idea is to tell pupils to put their hands up when they wish to ask a question, not to answer one. Then if a hand shoots up the teacher asks what question they wish to ask, and this quickly reminds them of the new rules.

'No hands up' demands that everybody should be ready with an answer; therefore, pupils must be asked a question that everyone can have an answer ready for. 'What do you think ...' and 'What do you know about ...' can be useful stems to start questions, as the answer 'I think that it is ...' will be correct if that is what they honestly think. 'No hands up' also demands that sufficient thinking time is allowed, so that the answers are what pupils really think or know and not just their instantaneous reactions.

If a teacher adopts the 'no hands up' rule in their classroom then pupils will be able to listen more to one another and to the teacher. In a talking and learning classroom pupils and the teacher must listen to one another and use the ideas that others express to help them learn. At the start a teacher can use stems such as: 'What do you think about what [name] said?', 'Can you add anything to [name]'s answer?' and 'What comment would you make on what [name] said?' to encourage pupils to listen to one another and to build on one another's answers. As pupils become used to this way of working most teachers find that pupils want to comment or build on another pupil's contribution as they realize that this is a good learning tool.

Practical ways to construct rich questions and activities

Once the conditions are right in the classroom for exploring answers and talking through ideas then teachers will need questions and activities that are worth thinking about. The following are a few ideas for setting about finding and using questions that stimulate rich thinking.

Setting a question that doesn't work or where the answer is unexpected. Pupils expect that all questions have simple straightforward answers and therefore in their struggle to find such an answer they will reveal any misconceptions they have.

Examples:

1 $a + 2b = 12$
$5a = 20$
Pupils do not expect a and b to have the same value and therefore struggle to find a different value for b.

2 At Key Stage 4 (14–16 years old) it can be useful to set a trigonometry question that cannot be solved using right-angled triangles. As pupils explore the problem and find that they cannot solve it simply using the tools that they already have, they will establish

the need for the cosine or sine rules. They will set such extension ideas in context, establishing when they need to use complex rules and when the simpler ideas will serve best.

Asking questions that are turned around from the usual way. These are questions that ask pupils to put together the complete web of ideas that make up a concept and use them in a different way. If pupils talk through and explore such ideas together then they will be more confident that they can use concepts. Teachers can ask all pupils to tackle challenging work by offering varying degrees of support. If we shield pupils from exploring different ways of using the concepts or expect only the best pupils to tackle such 'difficult' problems then teachers will not help the majority to be confident users of mathematics.

Examples:

1   The mean of 5 numbers is 8. We know that four of the numbers are 4, 10, 15 and 6. Which number must be missing?
2   All these products are approximately equal to 1600. Which of them are less than 1600 and which are more than 1600?

42×41 44×43.2

38.2×39.7 38×44

37×40.3 420×3.7

   a)   Justify your answers.
   b)   Invent 5 more products that are approximately equal to 1600.
   c)   What about 44×36? Why is this difficult to tell?

Using three to five questions that encompass ideas in a topic in order to generate discussion on the answers. Carefully choosing three to five questions that quickly start to challenge pupils' ideas about the concept that they are learning about is not easy but makes sure that pupils really explore ideas and check for misconceptions. The thought that pupils only complete three to five questions in a lesson may be new to some teachers, but it is important. If the questions are chosen carefully and they are explored and discussed together then pupils will gain a true sense of successfully knowing all about a concept.

Small-group work

Questions that stimulate the pupils to talk about their ideas to one another and help one another learn do not have to be whole-class questions. Sometimes the questions take the form of small-group activities. Pupils must be told that they are expected to articulate their ideas, use mathematical language and work together to solve the problems. The teacher will need to actively observe as the pupils are working if they are to make such small-group work an Assessment for Learning approach. The following are a few ideas.

Write a few questions on a card covering several aspects of a topic, possibly using exam questions if this is appropriate. The mark scheme for the questions would be written on a different-coloured card, which the pupils can refer to whenever they want. The purpose of the exercise is to support pupils as they learn how to answer challenging problems. They work together so that they discuss the how and why of the process of arriving at a correct solution.

Ask the pupils to look at the syllabus, framework or scheme of work and decide on an area that they feel they need to explore further. Point them to where they will find information on that area and ask them to write their own questions and mark scheme. Ask the pupils to give the questions to another group to answer, then mark them using their mark scheme. Using this idea enables two groups to fully explore the nuances of a particular area of mathematics, useful for revision but also in an area where there are several categories to explore or where it is a good idea to offer differentiated work, types of triangle, statistical graphs, and so on.

Explore links between questions in a standard exercise. Make use of the old textbooks in the cupboard; ask the pupils to look at the questions to explore why the book has asked certain questions, what system has been used to make the later questions harder or where challenge has been introduced in the way the question has been asked. Ask the pupils to write their own questions to form a similar, but possibly more interesting, exercise. This idea is very useful with pupils who are successful learners of mathematics, particularly in Years 12 and 13, but I have seen it used effectively with younger pupils who do not find mathematics easy. It encourages pupils to explore and articulate mathematical ideas; it encourages them to learn.

The common thread that runs through all these approaches is to ask pupils to think around all sides of the concept and to see, articulate and use all the complex web of ideas encompassed by it. The traditional route of learning to use one aspect then another harder aspect, then another and so on, can leave a pupil thinking that all the aspects are discrete and that there are no links between them. The pupils will need to learn about these different aspects but maintaining an overview of the whole concept is important as well. One way is to ask a 'Big Question' that, at the start, pupils have very little knowledge about how to solve. As they learn the different ideas, they can explore the 'Big Question' further until at last they can solve it and even make up their own 'Big Questions' for their peers to solve.

Feedback

Feedback is a vital component of Assessment for Learning. It is by obtaining and using feedback that pupils are able to know both what they have done well and how to continue to improve their learning. Pupils receive feedback in many ways, from the offhand 'that's a good way of putting it' from a peer to formal written feedback from a teacher. Learning objectives and success criteria enable pupils to feed back to themselves about their learning successes and where to go next to improve their learning. In a classroom where pupils use talk to learn about their mathematical ideas, feedback about their learning becomes part of the ongoing discourse.

This is not to suggest that all feedback assists learning. Feedback is only formative (that is, helpful to learning), if the information fed back to the learner is used by the learner in improving their learning. Feedback that is not understood by the learner, or cannot be acted on because there is no time to do so, is not going to improve learning, however helpful it is intended to be. Therefore, written feedback given at the end of a module of work will not be formative as a pupil cannot use it to improve their learning performance. It is also not enough to feed back to the pupil where they have misunderstood or otherwise found problems. To be formative it must tell the pupil how to improve; that is, it must specifically suggest actions that the pupil can take and they must act on those suggestions.

The work of Ruth Butler (1988) shows that it is important to separate comments from marks and grades if teachers are aiming to improve learning. Giving marks alongside the comments completely obliterates the beneficial effects of the comments. The use of both marks and comments is probably the most widespread form of feedback used in the United Kingdom. This study and others like it show that this practice, which takes up so much teacher time, does not help pupils to learn. When a pupil is given a grade it focuses them on their performance rather than their learning, and can demotivate or induce complacency. If a pupil regularly receives good grades they may become complacent as there is nothing to indicate that they need to continue to make an effort in their learning. Poor grades may convince pupils that they cannot 'do' mathematics, so it is not worth trying. Comments, without grades or marks, can identify what has been done well and point out what pupils' next steps are in their learning. Everybody can have such a comment on their work so that everyone, regardless of where they are, moves forward with their learning.

So what is effective feedback?

Effective feedback helps pupils to know how to move forward with their learning. This means that sometimes the most useful feedback for a student is a comment that allows them to spend time thinking through, and possibly talking about, the task that they have to do, as in the following example.

When a pupil is given a new task they often ask for help immediately. When the teacher asks, 'What can't you do?' it is common to hear the reply, 'I can't do any of it.' The pupil's reaction may be caused by anxiety about the unfamiliar nature of the task, and support can be provided by saying something like 'Copy out that table, and I'll be back in five minutes to help you fill it in.' This is often all the support the student needs. Copying out the table forces the student to look in detail at how the table is laid out, and this 'busy work' can provide time for them to make sense of the task for themselves. In this way, the teacher is providing a way for the pupil to move forward with their learning by giving permission to take time out to think.

There are three conditions for feedback to be effective. Whether oral or written, learners must know:

1   the learning objectives and success criteria for the task
2   the extent to which they have achieved the learning objectives/success criteria
3   how to move closer to achieving the learning objectives or how to close the gap between what they have done and what they could do.

The oral feedback above fulfils these conditions, if you assume that the teacher had spent time making sure that the learning objective and success criteria were clear and that the pupil had self-assessed the current extent to which she had achieved them (in this case, 'I can't do any of it'). The teacher provides the third condition: how to move closer to achieving the learning objective. Feedback does not have to be lengthy to be effective but it does have to help pupils move forward with their learning.

However, the three conditions do have their own difficulties when a teacher is starting to try and provide effective feedback. I have dealt with setting out the learning objectives and success criteria earlier. One of the reasons that success criteria are so important is that they can let pupils know how far they have been successful. It is vital that pupils know that they are successful learners, as only then will they know that it is worth trying to continue to improve. Success criteria allow pupils to work out for themselves *what* they have achieved and therefore *that* they have achieved. Where pupils have made the effort to learn, that effort will immediately be rewarded by referring to the success criteria. Where pupils are routinely using language to express their ideas they will be able to articulate to what extent they have met the success criteria, and therefore both teacher and pupils will share an immediate celebration of success. Where pupils cannot articulate their learning, recognition of successful learning will, at best, be delayed, and this will undermine its effect.

A comment detailing what has been successfully learned is an important start but it must be followed with a comment on what the pupil is to do to continue to improve. The phrasing of these 'improvement' comments is important. As a result of the comment the pupil must know what to do and how to do it. Exactly how this is achieved depends on the teacher, the pupil and the situation. Some suggestions include using comments that:

- remind the pupil of the learning objective or certain success criteria; these especially suit good learners, for example:
  - *Remember what happens when you multiply two negative numbers*
  - *Add an explanation of how to find the square root to complete your answer*
  - *You have forgotten to multiply by the coefficients of x*
- scaffold the pupils' answers; the teacher decides what method she thinks will enable the pupil to successfully solve the problem and directs them to it; she may then ask questions that will allow the pupil to think through the answer for themselves; teachers will often write out the solution with blanks for the pupil to fill in and then set a further problem for the pupil to solve in the same way:
  - *Use chunking to solve this problem*
  - *Do you think that the length of this side is right? Should it be longer or shorter than the other sides? How do you use Pythagoras' theorem to find a short side?*
  - $(2x - 3)(3x + 4) = \_\_x^2 + 8x - 9x - \_\_ = _____$, *now multiply* $(2x - 4)(3x + 2)$
- give an example and then ask the pupil to choose a way to use it:
  - *Use a table to work out the values for your graphs. What numbers will you choose for x when you draw your graphs?*

x	−5	−1	0	2
$y = x + 3$	−2	2		

  - *Describe what happens as your number pattern increases. Each next term will be something like 'double the one before it', 'three more than the one before it', 'three times the one before plus one'.*

These types of comments are by no means exhaustive; however, comments must:

- be focused on the learning goals, not the pupil
- be about the learning that should be going on, not only the presentation
- be clear about what the pupil has achieved and what still needs further work to improve
- demand a response from the pupil and be phrased so that they can understand how they should respond.

It is important to remember that research has found that feedback makes performance worse when it is focused on self-esteem or self-image, as is the case with grades and some ways of giving praise (Dweck 2000, Kluger and DeNisi 1996). The use of praise can increase motivation, but then it becomes necessary to use praise all the time to maintain that motivation. In this situation, it is very difficult to maintain praise as genuine and sincere. It is important to value specifically the pupil's effort in learning and what they have learnt well as this also raises their motivation to continue to learn. Improvement in performance results from feedback that is focused on what needs to be done to improve and specific details about how to improve.

Once the feedback is given there is another step to take before it becomes formative: the pupil must act on or make a response to the feedback. Once again, this is a time issue. Without time to read and respond to written feedback pupils will not value it. Therefore, when teachers have 'marked the books' they should make sure that at some time during the next lesson, probably at the start, the pupils read and begin to respond to the improvement advice given. Depending on the comment, pupils might:

- check that they understand what has been written and make a note to respond as homework
- read the comment and respond immediately as the comment will take only a short time to act on
- read the comment and redraft work that has been started, improving the work in the way suggested
- read the comment and feel unsure about how to respond so decide to talk to a peer to make sure that they do fully understand
- read the comment and complete two or three similar problems to show that they have understood the suggestion made
- find the four errors that they made in their work and write a reply to the teacher that shows that they understand where they had been going wrong.

Giving pupils effective written feedback will always take more time that the conventional 'ticking interspersed with random "goods"', as one girl called this style of marking. However, the conventional 'ticking'-type marking has no learning function, whereas a comment that sets out what has been done well and how the pupil is to continue to improve will help pupils to learn mathematics more effectively. Remember that in a classroom that focuses on using language to learn mathematics, pupils will be receiving feedback much of the time. As they hazard an idea in class or group discussion they will quickly find out if it is a good idea or not and hear some other good ideas to use. As they talk through their own ideas with one another they will 'hear' their own thoughts and this is a valuable way to check that their ideas make sense. By thinking and talking about their learning, pupils regularly receive feedback from the teacher and their peers and receive it at the right time – when they are struggling to understand a concept. However, schools demand written feedback as well, which pupils need to receive when they complete a written task as this ensures that everyone receives considered advice on how to move their learning forward. Therefore, time must be found. Teachers have devised many solutions to finding sufficient time to give effective feedback. These include:

- giving written feedback only every three weeks, but making sure every pupil gets some good advice when the feedback is given
- planning exactly which pieces of work should be given written feedback and which will be marked in class in some way; the work that will receive feedback from the teacher is often termed 'key pieces of work'
- only spending time writing comments when the advice will make a difference to pupils' learning, that is, when the pupils will have the time and the opportunity to act on the comments given
- marking routine work in class and spending teacher time only on work that really explores the learning that the pupil has been doing
- discussing ideas of quality with the pupils in class; part of this will involve looking at, assessing and commenting on the quality of one another's work
- marking work in small groups; the pupils use a set of model answers to investigate whether their answers are the same as the model answers and correct, different but still correct, or different and incorrect in some way; they then have to set out their own next steps in their work.

Peer and self-assessment

Peer assessment and self-assessment are important forms of assessment that engage pupils in talking about their learning and therefore help them to become self-critical and independent. They are not replacements for teacher marking and feedback. As with all areas of learning mathematics, pupils need to learn how to talk about their learning, the language and expressions to use in critiquing others' work and how to discuss problems and strategies with one another. This will take time and effort but the rewards are worthwhile. The pupil has to be an active agent in appraising and then closing the gap between their understanding at the outset and the objective of the learning, which means that effective learning must involve self-assessment by the pupil.

The act of talking about ideas and concepts makes those ideas available for feedback, from the teacher, from peers or from the pupils themselves. Provided that feedback is about the learning objective, identifies what has been done well and sets out ways to improve, it will help pupils to learn more. Peer assessment helps pupils learn the skills of self-assessment and also provides a rich resource of ideas that pupils can use in their own learning. When a group of pupils are engaged in peer assessment, the group will be talking about mathematical ideas and making and sharing meanings about those ideas. Each member will be part of the group's articulation of ideas and strategies and will thereby begin to internalize both the language and the ideas that are used. Peer and self-assessment provide a framework for talking about learning and therefore encourage meta-cognition, that is, thinking and talking about how and what pupils are learning.

Engaging in peer and self-assessment enables pupils to become self-reliant learners; they can guide their own learning because they know what they are trying to achieve and what they have to do to get there. Through peer and self-assessment, pupils become involved in the analysis and constructive criticism of their own work and this increases their rates of progress and levels of attainment. Pupils become able to focus their learning on the areas in which they feel they have the least confidence. They can pinpoint which parts/concepts in the topic give the most difficulty and concentrate their efforts where it will help most. Peer and self-assessment also enable teachers to learn more quickly and accurately about their pupils' ideas or difficulties and give them a deeper understanding of all pupils' progress and problems. Teachers can then decide where their time is best employed, who can carry on and who needs particular input.

All pupils can be involved in peer and self-assessment. Even in schools for pupils with learning difficulties I know pupils who think about one another's work and give their peers feedback and thereby learn a great deal about their own work. Pupils studying mathematics at a high level value collaboration in what can sometimes seem a lonely enterprise. They want to learn more and know that they can sort out problems together. Peer assessment can be a useful tool to help pupils begin to use specific phrases and ways of expression, as they need them in order to feed back to one another.

Pupils may need to learn ways to appreciate their own progress as many pupils undervalue their own work. Peer assessment will help them develop a more accurate view of their own abilities. Most pupils are honest in their assessment of their own work, most of the time. However, some pupils do not like to admit that they are not coping and say they understand when they do not, and peer and self-assessment are important ways to help overcome this. Pupils need constant reassurance that they are learning, and that, when work appears difficult, this is when they are learning the most.

Pupils are often more honest and challenging with one another than the teacher would be or they would be to the teacher. I know of a pupil that tidied up his work instantly when a peer told him that it was unreadable. The newly organized notebook revealed a great deal more about the pupil's mathematical ability to both the teacher and himself. Pupils challenge one another more than a teacher would feel able to do. When they know what is possible, what they are aiming for and how to get there they can be very demanding of one another. The whole process enables pupils to become more objective about their own work and to build up an idea of the quality of work that they are able to achieve.

Issues in using peer and self-assessment

Learning objectives and success criteria must be explicit and transparent to pupils. Pupils must know what is to be learnt and how they will know that they have successfully completed that learning. This is true for all lessons. Success criteria enable pupils to monitor or self-assess their progress during a lesson. Where they are engaging in a longer learning episode the success criteria may be called assessment criteria, possibly linked to those of external examinations. Pupils may be given the assessment criteria or may devise the criteria for themselves as a class. Whatever they are, it is important that pupils fully understand the criteria and what is expected in order to fulfil them. Pupils may know about the criteria but have no vision of what quality of work is expected. Exemplar work can be useful in this regard; in this case, the pupils use the criteria to mark exemplar pieces of work before they start their own. Using exemplar work and using criteria to peer assess others' work helps to overcome barriers to learning.

Pupils need to be taught the skills of collaboration in peer assessment. Teachers cannot assume that pupils will know how to critique others' work; pupils will need help to know what will be helpful and what may not. For example, teachers can instruct that pupils' assessments of their peer's work must refer to the success criteria, or that they identify two things that have been done well and give one idea that would improve the work. Pupils will make appropriate comments if they use the success criteria as their starting point. The balance of two good things and one area for improvement helps to build confidence. It is important to notice what has been done well as these are things that should be repeated in subsequent work. It is also important that the feedback identifies what to improve and how learning can move forward. Once pupils understand the process of peer assessment they will know that they will benefit from being the assessor and being assessed and will use the ideas to help them to improve their own learning.

Time needs to be built in to allow these processes to be taught, practised and become embedded into normal classroom practice. Peer and self-assessment take time: time to learn the way that the teacher wants to organize the assessment, time for pupils to learn how to assess and give feedback, time to reflect and act on the outcomes, and discover what has been learnt. At first this will seem to take a long time, but it is time well spent. The outcome will be a self-reliant learner who has strategies to help them to understand the assessment criteria and who can identify for themselves their next steps in learning.

Practical ways to use peer and self-assessment

Ask pupils to decide on their level of confidence with their work. This is a quick way to ask pupils to self-assess but it is important to help them learn self-assessment skills and to create a supportive ethos in the classroom. There are two main ways that teachers can ask their pupils to assess their level of confidence with their work: 'traffic lights' and 'thumbs up'. Whichever method is used, the teacher is asking for a quick assessment of whether each pupil in the class is confident that they understand the concept that they are learning about (green or thumbs up), still a little unsure (amber or thumb horizontal) or very unsure (red or thumbs down). The assessment can be made directly after the introductory discussion, to see who can get started straight away or who may need more discussion, or as a mini plenary during independent working, so that the teacher can use her time effectively. Once pupils get used to this way of working they can let their teacher know quickly if they are feeling unsure or need to look at a concept in a different way. Pupils seem to prefer to say 'I'm going a bit red on this' rather than 'I'm finding this difficult.' Pupils can 'traffic light' their work at the end of a lesson so that teachers can plan the next lesson to help those who need it and extend the learning of those that are feeling confident.

Create response partners. One of the most common ways that I see peer and self-assessment used is with response partners or study buddies. These are pairs of pupils that are chosen by the teacher either to work together all the time or to be assessment partners that check one another's work and offer ways to improve. Often the pairs are not friends. They are chosen to be critics, to talk together in order to identify for each other what has been done well and what still needs improvement and work out how that improvement will be made. It is important that there is a clear agreement and set of principles in place for how the partners are to work together. Teachers who use this method frequently display these rules and principles in the classroom so that they are a constant reminder of the expectations of the partnership. Some teachers ask pupils to get together with their partners for specific peer assessment tasks. Others use them in less formal ways; they may tell their pupils 'if you are stuck go and have a conversation with your response partner see if talking to them will help'. Response partners can start the important process of pupils learning to listen in order to learn from one another. In a classroom that uses language to learn mathematics listening is vital, and using response partners will develop pupils' knowledge of how important it is.

Use exemplar pieces of work. There are two main ways that teachers can use exemplars to develop pupils' understanding of how to assess their peers' and their own efforts.

One way is to use actual pieces of work – for example, last year's pupils' coursework.

Listed below are some common conventions.

- The work should be anonymous. Pupils can find it hard to critique others' work and anonymous work will remove one barrier.
- The success/assessment criteria can be provided by the teacher, drawn from pupils or externally provided, for example exam board criteria. It is not always necessary for it to be in 'pupil friendly' language as part of the purpose of the exercise is to learn the meaning of the language used in actual assessment criteria.
- The focus is on learning the full meaning of the success/assessment criteria, that is, coming to understand the quality of work required to achieve the criteria. Therefore, teachers often ask their pupils to assess three different pieces of work. The pieces will show pupils various ways to address the assessment criteria.
- Pupils work in small groups of three or four. The groups encourage pupils to articulate and therefore consolidate their understanding of what it means to meet each criterion.
- It is very important that pupils see a good piece of work – for example, a high-scoring piece of exam coursework or a well-crafted poster showing transformations of graphs. This will enable them to have a vision of how they can achieve a high standard themselves. It may be worth exploring poor quality as well; articulating why a piece of work is below standard will help pupils remember not to offer such pieces themselves.

- Pupils decide together where each piece of work has met the criteria and then decide on some advice for how it can be improved. Both these stages are important. The pupils' attention must be directed at the good points in order to know how to produce good work themselves and, by offering improvement advice, they will be articulating for themselves how to produce high-quality work.

Teachers can also ask pupils to assess exemplar work that contains common misconceptions and errors. This helps pupils to learn the skills of peer assessment while talking about their mathematical learning. Often teachers produce this type of work themselves. For example, they draw a graph with an inconsistent scale on the y-axis and plot points badly, or they make a 'mistake' when working with angles in a triangle and end up with an obtuse angle when the answer should be acute. Pupils are asked to consider the answers and to say what has been done correctly and then construct an explanation of how the work can be improved. This is a quick way to use peer assessment and can be done as a whole class. It helps to develop skills of peer assessment and helps pupils to learn to articulate their understanding. However, the focus here is on work that has not been done well and the exercise should not take much time so that pupils can quickly return to thinking about and producing high-quality work.

Marking homework with clear criteria. Peer assessment can be a useful tool to ensure that homework is completed. Homework, at its best, should be preparation for the next lesson and not a chore set independently of the rest of the work. If homework is set to check pupils' understanding of a concept, then the teacher will want to know at the start of the next lesson how successful they have been. All work should have clear criteria for successful completion and these can be used for peer assessment. Teachers should ensure that work is exchanged between pupils who do not normally work together. There will be less emotional involvement, making it easier for the pupils to be honest and straightforward. The peer assessor marks the work according to the criteria, identifying what has been done well and what needs to be improved. If the homework has not been done at all then the peer assessor will complain bitterly about this and this is usually sufficient to get the work done next time. The teacher observes closely while this is done and then questions the class about what they found. In about 10 minutes both the teacher and the class know what learning is needed next and why that decision has been taken – they are ready to go on learning.

Ask pupils to mark each other's work without giving them the answers. Although the pupils will find this difficult at first, asking them to work together to use textbooks, notes and one another's answers to decide on how well a peer has answered a problem is a useful tool. It teaches the pupils both that they have resources at their disposal and how useful those resources are. Working together, groups are usually able to come up with good solutions and to explain where they need to improve their own answers.

Introduce 'four square' peer and self-assessment. This method of using peer and self-assessment is useful when pupils will be engaged in a lengthy task that will take several lessons to complete. At the start of the task pupils take an A4 sheet of paper and fold it into quarters. They will record the success/assessment criteria in the top-left 'square'; the other three 'squares' will be used for peer assessment later. About two-thirds of the way through the time allocated for the task, pupils swap work with their response partner or a peer assessor chosen by the teacher. The peer assessor uses the assessment criteria to fill in the top-right 'square' with 'what has been done well'. The peer assessor also fills in the bottom-left square with 'what needs to be improved', again using the criteria to decide what to write. The work is then returned and each pupil reads the advice that they have been given and considers what they have found out by assessing someone else's work. The final square is the 'me square'; here they record what they have learned about how to continue to improve their work and use those notes to make the necessary enhancements.

The four square

Success criteria	What has been done well?
What needs to be improved?	Me

The improvement matrix. This is a way for pupils to think about their work and to set out criteria that will help them to produce the very best results that they can.

The improvement matrix

	Communication	Systematic working	Use of algebra	Use of graphs and diagrams
Well above standard				
Above standard				
Acceptable standard				
Below standard				

At the start of the time allocated for the work the class discuss how they could describe a piece of work where the communication was acceptable, below standard, above standard or well above standard. Exemplar pieces of work could be used to help pupils devise the descriptions. The headings in the matrix above were devised for a piece of coursework in order to focus pupils on working systematically, using algebra appropriately and using diagrams efficiently. Pupils may need to have some idea of how they are going to investigate a problem before they can complete the matrix, so rather than complete it all at once they could be asked to complete one section in each of four lessons. Two-thirds of the way through they could then use their improvement matrix to peer assess others' work. The matrix can also be used in the final summative marking process.

Conclusion

Developing Assessment for Learning and developing pupils' ability to use language to express their mathematical ideas must go hand in hand. It is important that pupils express what they really know, understand and can do if Assessment for Learning is to be used effectively. However, in mathematics, articulating ideas can be very difficult and understanding can be masked by an inability to express them. When teachers help their pupils to become better able to express their mathematical ideas they will also help them to consolidate those ideas. When pupils can confidently express a mathematical concept then they know that they can use and control it, and their teacher also knows where to go next in order to continue to improve that learning.

Assessment for Learning is fully embedded in a classroom that talks about what they are learning, and how they are learning, and uses that discourse to make and share meaning. In such classrooms questioning is used to explore understanding, thinking time is given and both the teacher and the pupils actively listen to the answers. The pupils receive feedback which helps them understand where they have been successful in their learning and what the next steps are to move their learning forward. The pupils also engage in peer and self-assessment as this enables them to take a meta-cognitive view of and responsibility for their learning.

When Assessment for Learning is embedded as a part of mathematics classroom practice, pupils are able to be self-efficacious, they know how to learn and self-regulate, they can steer their own learning, and their self-esteem and therefore their motivation – is high. They know that they are able to be successful learners.

5 Going further with purposeful communication in mathematics

In this chapter I will talk more about involving all the pupils in the learning process. If pupils are to improve the standard of their learning in mathematics then they need to talk about mathematics more. By communicating their ideas as they learn they will become able to use and control mathematical concepts with more confidence than they presently do. However, the pupils must take on a different role in the mathematics classroom and so must the teacher. Pupils must be involved in and responsible for their own learning and teachers must help them to be able to do this. Teachers can accomplish this in several ways: by changing the ways in which pupils interact with the work and each other; by giving them more challenging problems to solve; and by asking them to express their mathematical ideas in writing. I discuss all these issues in this chapter.

Involving the pupils in the learning process

Being involved in the learning process means that the pupils feel ownership of the process and have some control over the way their learning proceeds. For instance the pupils may control what idea they wish to pursue, how they complete a task or even the pace of lessons. The pupils are involved when they take a full part in the classroom discourse. The more that pupils are involved in the process of learning mathematics, the more successful they will be, because they will:

- be able to talk about the mathematics that they are learning, thereby knowing which concepts they are able to understand and use and which they still have to learn, and how to go about improving
- be able to take responsibility for their own learning, knowing where there are gaps and how to close them

- have a vision of what they are aiming to achieve and how to get there
- feel ownership in the process, thereby remaining more interested and more motivated
- develop an intuitive knowledge of the criteria for success in their work, resulting in much greater task perseverance even when they find the work difficult.

Focusing on language in mathematics aims to allow the pupils to take control over their own mathematical thoughts and ideas. Facilitating pupils' ability to express their mathematical ideas is a big step towards securing their involvement in the learning process.

Pupils learn more effectively when they understand their responsibility for the outcome of the learning process. When pupils take on responsibility for their own learning they see the teacher as a resource to help their learning. The teacher's role becomes that of facilitator or enabler, not imposing or intruding but supporting and nurturing. Pupils became involved in this way when the teacher negotiates with them the way that the lesson should proceed and when the discourse is about the content that the pupils are to learn and also about the way that they should go about that learning. When pupils take a full part in a discussion, affecting the course of the discussion and being affected by it, they go away from that discussion able to use the ideas that had been discussed. When the pupils are involved in the learning process, they become an integral part of discourse that develops knowledge; they become part of a meaning-making community. Pupils' involvement in the work means that they are encouraged to take a meta-cognitive stance, they maintain an awareness of their own learning and are able to take responsibility for it.

All the ideas in the previous two chapters are aimed at involving the pupils in the learning process. However, in this chapter I would first like to deal with three more areas that I have not yet discussed:

1   small-group work, which can be challenging in mathematics but which is vital if the pupils are to feel involved
2   allowing the pupils to make choices in their work, an important factor in enabling the pupils to take responsibility for their own learning
3   encouraging the pupils to act as teachers, an approach that allows pupils to know that they know about and can use and explain mathematical ideas.

Working in small groups

Small-group work is very important in a talking and learning mathematics classroom. If the pupils talk as a whole class, each pupil receives a great variety of input from other people but there is little time for their own contribution. Organized small-group work is, therefore, an important feature of a mathematics classroom where all the pupils learn to talk about their mathematical ideas. They have to 'think aloud' when they work together in groups, trying out ideas and receiving feedback from one another. The act of vocalizing an idea can in itself allow the person saying it to know how important it is or to know if it does not quite make sense. Small-group work allows more of the pupils the advantages of being able to think aloud themselves and to hear others thinking aloud.

The first and most important consideration is that the effective interaction in small groups does not just happen; like everything else in school, the pupils have to learn how to interact and how to learn together. When small-group work is set up carefully the pupils will learn a great deal from being part of the process.

It is important to consider the following principles when using small-group work.

Small-group work is not three or four pupils doing the same work sitting together at a table; when the pupils are taking part in groupwork they each have a specific role within that group and a responsibility to the group to fulfil their own task. The purpose of working and talking together, each adding their own experience and insight, is to create something that is greater than each individual could have created alone.

The groupwork task is introduced by explaining to the pupils why they are working in small groups. The plenary is used for reflection on the mathematics learned and on their group working experience so that they consider how their behaviour in a group working situation has contributed to the success, or otherwise, of the task.

Groups must be 'purposeful' groups, that is they must be chosen with a particular purpose in mind. For example, teachers may decide to put pupils who show good understanding of the task together with those who have some understanding and those with some understanding together with those who are having difficulty getting started so that every pupil has a chance to teach and learn from other pupils. They may decide to group pupils with a similar level of understanding in the topic together so that every pupil can be specifically challenged, or they may decide to use friendship groups because they know that the pupils will need to support one another due to the nature of the task. Whichever way teachers decide to group the pupils it must be planned along with the activity and the decision must be taken with a particular purpose in mind.

Llewellyn

Llewellyn was listed along with Troy as 'one of the lads'. He was sociable and chatty, but was not prepared to talk about mathematical ideas, probably because he was concerned not to look stupid in front of his friends.

He began to use mathematical language in whole-class discussions, tentatively at first. He listened to other people and during a lesson where I asked the pupils to think of any words they knew that were associated with percentages Llewellyn began to show that he was prepared to try to use mathematical language.

'After suggesting all the usual words, Colette suggested ratio and immediately Llewellyn suggested fraction.'

Llewellyn listened to other people and used their thoughts to extend his own. Fairly soon he began to help out other people if they were unsure.

'Shaun said, at first, that he had got it wrong because he had answers such as 0.6857892. But Llewellyn said "but that's 0.7 isn't it Miss?"'

The pupils worked in small groups when they were exploring mathematical problems. Sometimes I was able to enter into their discussions and further encourage their use of mathematical ways of expression. When Llewellyn was completing his Golf Ball Project I witnessed him using mathematical language to 'think out loud':

'This is a big box to fit 12 in,' Llewellyn said pointing to a net he had drawn for a 10 x 3 x 3 cuboid. 'So how many will fit along here?' I asked 'Three in ten centimetres' 'And here?' 'One, oh I see, not enough … I see what I've done wrong!'

Later Llewellyn commented, without prompting, *'how much more confident he feels in Maths now. He feels he has worked hard.'*

Llewellyn came to see himself as a successful learner in mathematics. At the end of the year, it was clear that he saw himself as able to use and control mathematical ideas and was willing to get involved in the work that he was doing and to complete it well. He knew how to use mathematical language to 'think out loud' and enable him to organize his thoughts and solve mathematical problems. He also saw himself as able to help out other people in their struggle to understand.

The activity must warrant working together in groups; there must be a reason to discuss the work and contribute to the evolving knowledge of the group. Examples of suitable tasks are:

- putting together some individual research on patterns in the equations of transformed graphs, or on the properties of certain geometrical shapes, as each person will have specific knowledge to contribute and knowledge to gain from the others in the group
- working together as a group to ascertain the correct solution to a homework question when the answers are not provided
- comparing their own solutions to a lengthy problem to that provided by the teacher; the group have to decide together whether their own solutions are correct and the same, correct but different, or incorrect, and decide what errors have been made
- considering a series of problems on cards and deciding whether the answers will be found using the sine ratio, the cosine ratio, or the tangent ratio; the task is not to answer the questions but to talk about how to answer them.

In each of the above tasks the group need to share their existing knowledge and experience in order to complete the task; they must work together, talk and share their ideas as the task would be excessively difficult for one person to complete on their own.

The teacher must make explicit to the pupils that they are expected to work together and how they are expected to do so. Teachers often assume that pupils know how to talk and work together, but pupils may think that using one another's ideas is 'cheating' or that they are not 'allowed' to talk and share their ideas. Such ideas should be becoming less prevalent, especially in the UK where the National Strategy is promoting working and thinking together, but I still hear of them from pupils and teachers. Pupils will get most benefit from working together as a group when the work is challenging. If the group work together and pool their ideas then they will be able to support one another and master difficult work. However, it can be hard for the pupils to remember to work together if the work has unsettled them. It is vital, therefore, that the teacher sets out how they are expected to work together until absolutely sure that the class supports one another as second nature.

If small-group work is set up according to the above principles then pupils will benefit greatly from working together, sharing ideas and being able to articulate and receive feedback on their own mathematical ideas. Pupils who regularly explore mathematical ideas in this way talk and learn together even when not explicitly instructed to do so because they understand how helpful it is.

Woodside Maths Department
Group Talk Rules
- ◆ Everyone must contribute – do not rely on just one person.
- ◆ Express your own ideas clearly.
- ◆ Respect everyone's contribution.
- ◆ Listen carefully to one another.
- ◆ Give one another feedback .
  tell them if you think their idea is good
  tell them if you can see a way that their idea could be improved
  tell them if you think they have made a mistake, but be prepared to explain and to listen to them.

Choice is important

Pupils must be able to make choices if they are to take responsibility for their own learning and know that they are involved in the learning process. Pupils become involved in the learning process by being offered choice and being encouraged to make some decisions about the learning that they do. Pupils do welcome choice but do not always find it easy to exercise it. Therefore, teachers must help their pupils know that there are choices to be made and that they are capable of making them. Here are some examples of choices.

What learning work to do. For example, the teacher will provide three different ways for the pupils to continue to improve their knowledge about quadratic equations. Those who feel comfortable with the work so far and are ready to go further will choose one way, those who need a little more practice but are fairly confident will choose another way and those who still feel uncertain will choose the third way. The teacher does not make the choice or even advise the pupils; the consequence for the pupil in making a wrong choice is that they will have the wrong work to do. It is the pupils' responsibility to learn and therefore their responsibility to make the right choice. They can change their mind and choose differently when they have seen the work. The learning intention in this lesson is partly to improve the pupils' ability to use quadratic equations and partly to emphasize the pupils' central role in the learning process.

How to do the learning work. When pupils are engaged in investigating a mathematical problem they will be able to choose how to pursue the problem and even when they have investigated enough. The pupils will find such a wealth of choices difficult unless they have become used to making choices in other lessons. Therefore, being asked to make small choices about how to do the learning work will help the pupils become better at making bigger choices; for example, 'Do you want to use the whiteboards to write that down or would you prefer just to talk about it?'

'Do you want to try drawing these graphs first or will you go straight on to answering the Big Question?'

What mathematical concept to use. The pupils should be able to decide which mathematical concept is appropriate to solve a particular mathematical problem. This is an important skill when it comes to passing examinations but it is also an important life skill. When pupils are asked to make choices about what mathematics to use, they come to know that they are capable of making those choices. In whole-class discussion the pupils can be presented with a question and asked to make suggestions about how to solve it. This approach can be used frequently, especially if the question is chosen carefully. Sometimes the pupils have to choose between ideas that the class has recently studied, other times they have to choose ideas that have been studied a long while ago. The approach always asks the pupils to describe the process of getting to the answer and why they have chosen one way rather than another. In small-group work the pupils can be presented with small cards bearing different word problems. Depending on the pupils' learning stage, these could be anything from arithmetic problems that ask the pupils to choose whether they would use addition, subtraction, multiplication or division to problems that involve the various forms of integration. Again, the point is that the pupils focus on choosing the appropriate mathematical concept, looking for clues and articulating and making informed decisions, not on solving the problem.

How quickly to move on to more or different work. It is important that the pupils know that they should take some share in decisions about when they have learned a concept and are ready to take on more or different work. They are the ones that are doing the learning and, therefore, they should be able to express their opinion about the state of their learning. Learning objectives and success criteria will help the pupils to make these decisions, but unless the pupils are involved in a discussion about the pace of the learning the teacher will be acting on previous experience. With help pupils will be able to express their feeling on the pace of their learning and then the teacher will be able to say to him/herself, 'I no longer have to guess, they tell me what they need to learn'.

Involving pupils in the teaching process

Pupils can become involved in the learning process by being part of the teaching process. When pupils help one another to learn about mathematical ideas they naturally take on the identity of a mathematician, that is, someone who can talk about mathematical concepts and therefore knows about and can use them.

Pupils can become part of the teaching process in several ways – even when they correct one another in a discussion they are taking part in the teaching process. In the following exchange from a discussion at the end of a lesson Llewellyn was taking on a teaching role. He knew about rounding decimals and he knew about the tangents the class were exploring.

> Shaun said, 'I've got it wrong; my answers are all like, 0.6857892,' Llewellyn said 'but that's 0.7 isn't it Miss?'

> Following this exchange Llewellyn went and sat by Shaun and checked that he had understood. When pupils take a full part in the discourse of a classroom, they become able to express their understanding of mathematical concepts and are therefore able to take on the role of teacher. When Llewellyn explained to Shaun that he had got the right idea and that he could use tangents to solve problems, Llewellyn had to articulate his ideas clearly using the mathematics register and he deepened his understanding of tangents. Shaun had someone who talked about the work at his level and who could give him the time that he needed to ask questions. In this situation both Shaun and Llewellyn benefited.

As the pupils articulate their mathematical ideas more fluently they are more able, and therefore more likely, to act as teacher in an informal way. It is possible to set up more formal activities where the pupils are required to act as teacher to one another. This will have the same benefits that I have described above. The 'teacher-pupil' will be required to articulate their understanding clearly and accurately, forcing them to examine the mathematical concept in depth and often to reach a deeper and more full understanding. The 'learner-pupil' will have a 'teacher' who talks to them at their level, has some understanding of the problems they are going through and who they may feel they can ask questions which they would not ask their teacher. Here are two ideas for asking the pupils to act as teachers.

1   Ask the pupils to traffic light themselves on how confident they feel with the concept that they are learning about. Ask the 'green' people (those who feel confident) to work with the 'amber' people (those who feel a little unsure) to answer any questions that they have so that they all end up 'green'. The teacher goes to work with the 'red' people (those who feel very unsure) to help them with their problems.

2   After marking a piece of work, pair up pupils on the basis of their success, high with medium and medium with lower. The responsibility of the 'teacher' is to enable the 'learner' to succeed with more of the work, for example to achieve 5 more marks on a 'mock' exam paper. It is important to impress on the pupils that the 'learner' must understand how to succeed with more of the work, not just be given the answers.

Challenge is an issue in pupils' learning

Challenge is an important factor in a talking and learning classroom. A task is challenging if it asks for mathematical thinking that is more complex than that which would normally be expected from the pupils. Consequently, a task that one pupil finds challenging another may not. A challenging task is difficult for a pupil to complete and engages the pupils in thinking about a concept for a length of time. The teacher needs to know her students in order to be able to set the mathematical challenge as high as it can be (Jaworski 1994, p. 96). I have found that when the challenge is high and the class talks, works and supports one another they can meet such challenges and will experience the great satisfaction that comes from mastering something that was difficult.

Once they become used to the idea, pupils enjoy working through one or two demanding problems in a lesson rather than rushing through many easier ones. When I surveyed pupils to find their views on this, most of them acknowledged that working hard to explore a complex problem was more beneficial to their learning than working through many short problems. There was one dissenting voice. His reason for preferring many short problems was that doing so was easier for him and did not require him to think. Pupils have to get used to a new way of thinking. They are used to success in mathematics being recognized by many 'ticks' in their books. When they spend the lesson working together to solve one 'Big Question' they may not write anything in their books at all. Success criteria will show the pupils that they are learning successfully and what they have successfully learnt. Here are a couple of things you can try.

Try setting three 'hard sums'. Ask the pupils to work in small groups to try and see how far they can get with each one, writing their ideas on A4 sheets of paper. Ask the groups to bring their attempts to the board and stick them where everyone can see all the attempts. Discuss the solution to each problem by looking at how each group started, how they continued and how the problem might be completed. Pool all the ideas generated from the group discussions, considering as a whole class which ideas may be helpful. Using the term 'hard sums' helps the pupils know that they are not expected to complete all the problems on their own and adds to the pupils' feeling of success when they come to understand how to solve them.

Try spending all lesson on one 'Big Question'. Start by looking at the problem and deciding what mathematical ideas will be needed to solve it. Check that the class can use all these ideas. Ask the pupils to start to solve the problem, calling everyone together several times to report on ideas for a solution, progress made and any further information that may be needed. Towards the end of the lesson ask one group to report on how they have solved the 'Big Question' and ask the rest of the class to question the reporting group on the process they went through or on anything that they feel has not been made clear. Discuss any differences in the way that other groups tackled or solved the problem.

Even the most careful teacher will occasionally set the level of challenge too high. This need not be a disaster. If a relationship of trust has developed between the teacher and the class then it is possible for the teacher to admit that he has misjudged and to discuss what the class needs to learn before they can tackle the challenging work. Once the missing concepts have been learnt then the class can return to the challenging question. It is important to establish 'harmony' (Potari and Jaworski 2002, p. 374), that is, a balance between sensitivity to pupils' learning needs and the mathematical challenge provided to aid their cognitive development.

Literacy and mathematics

Many people find it difficult to connect literacy and mathematics, but this whole book is about just that. Literacy is about being able to communicate your ideas clearly to other people and to understand what other people are trying to communicate to you. Therefore, learning to express your mathematical ideas, whether orally or in writing, is improving your literacy in mathematics.

In this section I am going to discuss writing in mathematics. So far I have not specifically considered writing, preferring the more ambiguous 'articulating or communicating mathematical ideas', which can of course mean speaking or writing. This is partly because in a busy classroom it is inevitable that writing will be used to ensure that every pupil's expression of a mathematical idea can be scrutinized by another member of the community. However, many of the ideas that I have discussed that involve writing suggest using scrap paper or whiteboards, so that the expressions are temporary. It is hard for the pupils to use mathematical language, hard to find the right words and hard to create the meaning that the pupil wants. Writing is in itself a barrier to many pupils. They find the act of writing hard and they are concerned by the permanence of the written word. Therefore, many pupils find writing down their mathematical ideas very difficult.

I do not suggest that pupils are not asked to write in mathematics; in fact, I would advocate that the pupils are asked to write at length, to explain and justify how to make use of mathematical ideas. However, teachers must not forget that this is a difficult thing to ask most pupils to do. It is also important that the pupils think and talk, and writing should not get in the way of these important activities. Pupils will need a great deal of support in producing any written mathematical communication. Chief amongst that support is being able to talk confidently about the ideas that they will subsequently commit to writing.

Purposeful writing and recording

Writing and recording in mathematics should have a purpose. Writing is often used as a matter of course in mathematics when in fact the pupils would learn more by thinking and talking together and making notes of their discussions in a temporary way. If there is no need to write then I would exhort mathematics teachers not to give in to any pressure they may perceive for the pupils to produce exercise books full of neat, correct sums. If a teacher does come under overt pressure to make pupils write when they feel they may learn more by thinking and discussing, then I would say 'let the results do the talking'. Seek permission to experiment with working in this way with one group and let the results after, say, a year (results do not come quickly when major changes in ways of working are made) decide if the pupils need to write everything down or not.

There are times when writing is important. Writing involves producing a permanent record of thought and ideas; therefore, any written record should be thought about at length and probably redrafted. One teacher asks his pupils to call the books in which they write their Personal Revision Guides. This emphasizes that by writing they are creating a permanent record of ideas and concepts in order to help them to recall those ideas at a later date. They are not doing 'exercises' so they do not call their books 'exercise books'.

Think, talk, write, read and re-draft

In this section I will use 'write' to mean making a permanent record of mathematical thoughts, ideas and concepts, as opposed to making notes or a transient record to aid thinking. Writing does have more of a place in mathematics classrooms than is often thought. Asking the pupils to make a permanent record of the ideas that they have been learning has all the benefits of articulating them. Ideas become ordered, confusions are uncovered and sorted out, misconceptions are addressed and the whole becomes more easily remembered and able to be used at other times to solve other problems. Writing makes a permanent record that can be reviewed at a later time and ideas that are written about can more easily be called to mind.

If writing has all the benefits, and more, of articulating mathematical ideas, then it has all the difficulties, and more, as well. The pupils are not only being asked to think and talk using language that they do not feel to be theirs, they are also being asked to make a record of those thoughts that others can see and therefore assess. It is unsurprising that pupils find requests for them to write about their mathematical ideas both daunting and difficult. Many teachers see this aspect as so difficult that they feel the benefits are not worth the costs. However, even if pupils never form an English sentence in mathematics, even if they are never asked to explain, describe or justify their ideas, they will be asked to form mathematical sentences. It is possible to view solutions to mathematical problems as paragraphs with the sentences in the correct order so that they make sense and result in an answer. Explaining, describing and justifying are an important part of mathematics; the system of thinking that is mathematics requires the communication of ideas. When pupils are asked to write as part of their mathematics lessons they are engaging in important areas of mathematical thinking.

Writing is important, but it is difficult and demanding in mathematics. Therefore, if writing is to be the final outcome of a learning experience the pupils must be supported as they engage in deciding on what to write. The support might take the form of talking about what is to be written and deciding as a whole class what important words and ideas should be included in the piece (in effect this sets out the success criteria). The pupils then work individually to produce a rough draft of what they want to say. They read their draft to a partner, who makes suggestions about anything that may be missing or does not seem to be clear. The teacher calls the class together and asks about any issues that came up in the discussions or anything that the pairs could not sort out on their own. Only then do the pupils produce their final written pieces.

A writing activity could also involve pupils working in pairs to devise a flowchart which details the sequence of events that must happen, the conditions that must apply and the decisions that must be made as a mathematical concept is used to solve a problem. The flowcharts are displayed and everyone looks at several other pupils' attempts. They use green highlighters to show ideas that they think are particularly good and orange highlighters to show areas that they think the pupils might have to review. The teacher looks closely at the flowcharts to find out if there are ideas or misconceptions that may have to be addressed for everyone, or for just a few pupils. The pupils retrieve their flowcharts and amend them in the light of the orange highlights, the teacher's feedback or because they saw another way that they felt was clearer than the way they had used. The flowchart may then be used to produce a written account with examples of the ideas that they have learned and clarified, or the pupils may just improve their flowchart and add some examples to it.

If the pupils are to make a permanent communication of their mathematical ideas then it is important that they:

Think	about what they are trying to communicate and be given time to do so.
Talk	to at least one other person, but preferably more, as they decide how to express their communication.
Write	only when they have thought and talked about their ideas.

Read   to themselves and to other people to see and hear whether they are communicating well.

Re-draft   based on feedback received from the reading stage, therefore learning both how to improve their work and that they can produce high-quality communications.

When and when not to write

In many mathematics lessons the pupils do too much writing and not enough thinking. The pupils do not think about the ideas that they are applying, in what circumstances they will work and when they will not. I advocate less writing and more thinking. More thinking will involve more talking, as talking is the way that people think together and more talking will help the pupils to be able to understand the full meaning of the concept under discussion and to use and control it fully.

There are, however, times when writing or recording ideas is important:

- when pupils need to make a permanent record of an idea that they have come to know well, so that they can refer to it later
- when a silent reflective time is appropriate so that the pupils can note down how much they understand of or can apply a concept
- when they set questions on a concept for someone else to do
- when they are trying to solve a complex problem with many steps and need a record of the routes they have taken
- when they are asked to explain to their teacher what they know, understand and can do, so that appropriate subsequent lessons can be planned
- when they need to transform some ideas that have been developed together as a class into reminders for themselves on how to apply a concept.

Examples of times when pupils do not need to write:

- when they should be thinking; writing can make pupils 'switch off' while they copy something into their books
- when they should be talking and clarifying their ideas rather than concentrating on the act of writing
- when they are solving simple sums for practice which would be better worked out in their heads and answers noted on a whiteboard or scrap paper if necessary
- when they are working together as a group to create a memorable explanation; the pupils need to talk and thrash out a convincing explanation; recording too soon may stop the struggle for concision and clarity which is part of mathematical thinking.

It may be worth thinking about writing as 'making talk more permanent'. When the pupils have thought and talked and clarified their ideas then they will be ready to write them down, further refining them as they strive to produce a clear, concise and accurate record of a mathematical concept. Their writing will then be useful as a record of what they need to know in order to use mathematical concepts or ideas. The pupils will be able to refer back to their writing and it will take them through the steps they need to solve a problem, using, for example, Pythagoras' theorem, in a way that looking at solved problems may not do. Their writing will thus perform two functions: the act will clarify and order their ideas and the record will allow them to refer back and use that concept later.

If teachers are helping their pupils to learn more easily by helping them to be able to talk about their mathematical ideas, then writing will be less of a feature of their classroom. The pupils will claim that they have 'done no work in maths' because they have not written in their exercise books, when in fact they will have worked hard – thinking, talking, reflecting, clarifying, explaining and justifying their thoughts and learning how to use and control mathematical ideas. They will be working very hard learning mathematical ideas that they will be able to use away from the mathematics classroom because they know and understand the concepts and can see how mathematical ideas connect together.

Conclusion

In this chapter I have talked more about involving the pupils in the process of learning. The more that pupils are asked to talk about mathematical ideas, to use mathematical words and expressions, the more they will be able to use, control and connect mathematical ideas and the more accurately they will assess their own ability to do so. Including all the pupils in the discourse of the classroom is not easy or straightforward and it takes time. Both the teacher and the pupils need to come to terms with their new role in the classroom. The teacher must learn to do less of the talking and thinking and take on a more managerial role, planning activities and setting the ethos so that the pupils can do more of the talking, thinking and learning. The pupils have to take an active role and become able to take on the responsibility to act to further their own learning.

6   The source of the ideas – delving into theory

Introduction

In this chapter I will explain the theoretical basis for the ideas contained in the previous chapters. I will explore why practice should change in the ways that I have advocated and also what the expected outcomes would be of such changes. I will link language and learning in mathematics using the available literature.

Theory demanded a change in my practice and I saw how this change empowered my pupils, and subsequently other teachers' pupils, to use and control mathematical ideas. I see a theoretical background as an important factor in sustained change; a teacher's basic beliefs have to assimilate the ideas if change is to be more than superficial. Exploring the theory presented here may challenge you to change, give you reasons to make changes in your classroom practice and stimuli to effect that change. However, change must be nurtured if it is to become embedded and I shall explore how that might happen in the later parts of this chapter.

First, I provide an overview of theory that connects language and learning and explore in some depth the specific links between mathematical language and learning. I define the term 'discourse community' and explain why it is useful terminology for a classroom where use of language is the paramount learning tool. I go on to explore some theoretical background to Assessment for Learning and briefly explore several theories of change.

An overview of the theory linking language and learning

In my view, the outcome of making the changes that I have put forward will result in the classroom becoming a 'discourse community' where the discourse is framed to further mathematical learning. Discourse has a variety of meanings and uses; here I use it to mean the processes through which groups of individuals communicate with one another (see for example Cazden 1986 and Pimm 1996a). Therefore, in a mathematics classroom discourse can include many features, such as an oral interchange of ideas or written responses from the teacher and the pupils. Discourse covers the whole range of language-based communication of ideas within the classroom that is 'language as it is used to carry out the social and intellectual life of a community' (Mercer 1995, p. 79).

I also use the term 'discourse community' as it seems to evoke the various facets of a classroom environment that are beneficial to improved mathematical learning. The term has been used for some years in the US, (see for example Wertsch and Toma 1995; Silver and Smith 1996; Sherin 2002). In particular, the term is used to describe a mathematics classroom that is acting in the way advocated by the National Council of Teachers of Mathematics (NCTM 1991), in 'supporting, doing and talking about mathematics'. Specifically in such communities pupils are expected to state and explain their ideas and respond to ideas voiced by other members of the class. Teachers act in a way that facilitates such conversations or interchange of ideas. The discourse in classrooms described in this way is 'diverse and plentiful' (NCTM 2000).

There is quite a history behind my call for more use of language in the learning of mathematics. The first issue of the National Curriculum for Mathematics (DfES 1989) required pupils to talk about their work and respond to and ask mathematical questions. This built on the Cockcroft Report (Cockcroft 1982), which argued for strategies that improved mathematical communication in the classroom, and the report 'Mathematics for Ages 5 to 16' which states, 'In its broadest sense mathematics provides a means for organizing, communicating and manipulating information. The language of mathematics consists of diagrams and symbols with associated conventions and theorems' (DES/WO 1988, p. 3). Language is central to learning mathematics; the better pupils are at using mathematical language, the better they will be able to show their mathematical knowledge. That is, they will be assessed as being better mathematicians. 'Mathematics education begins and proceeds in language, it advances and stumbles because of language and its outcomes are often assessed in language' (Durkin and Shire 1991, p. 1).

Morgan (1995) demonstrated that the way that pupils represent their personal mathematical activity in the texts they produce is potentially significant to their success in mathematics. Their ability to describe their reasoning and patterns that they observe in mathematical activities in a conventional mathematical style can be a factor in their success at Key Stage 3 (an examination taken at age 14 in England) and probably more importantly at GCSE (an examination taken at age 16 in England and Wales). If the pupils are able to write about the processes they used in producing mathematical coursework in a conventional impersonal style, their work will probably be assessed more positively than others describing the same mathematical processes without skill in the conventional style. Therefore, an ability to communicate information in a structured, precise way using the concise, impersonal style that is conventionally mathematical is important for pupils' success as mathematicians.

The theory that the pupils will be assessed as better mathematicians the better they are at using mathematical language is also predicated on the theories of Gergen (1995). He theorizes that the better pupils can use the discourse that mathematicians may use, the more they become 'mathematicians', that is, someone who can solve problems using mathematics. There are other theories that emphasize the importance of learning to speak like a mathematician in order to take on the identity of a mathematician (see for example Holland *et al.* 1998, Lave and Wenger 1991, Wenger 1999). The more pupils are able to 'talk like a mathematician' the more they will take on the identity of a 'mathematician', and, therefore, the more they will consider themselves, and be considered by others, to have learned mathematics. A facility with the language that is used to express mathematical ideas, therefore, is more than just desirable, it is part of becoming able to 'do' mathematics. It is the vehicle through which the pupils come to consider themselves as able to use and control mathematical concepts.

A classroom is a community that will have a particular culture created by the teacher and pupils and also by the subject being learned. Learning mathematics can be seen as becoming enculturated into mathematics. The 'scientific' or 'traditional' view of mathematics is that it is a fixed and unchanging body of knowledge, but actually mathematics is a tradition that is constantly being 'heard anew and reformulated' (Evans and Tsatsaroni 1994, p. 169) by a community of people who think about and develop the system of knowledge that is mathematics. Pupils can become enculturated into the mathematical community when they intentionally develop new mathematical ways to organize their experience or reflect on the organization, strategies and concepts that they have already developed. This may consist of a search for patterns and consistency, or an attempt to generalize or formalize procedures, make connections within the system and develop logical arguments to use to prove and to share their results. These practices, because they have an origin in language, may be called discursive practices.

Mathematical language and theories of learning

Discussion of the theories of learning must begin with radical constructivism, as explained by von Glaserfeld (1984), who built on the work of Piaget. Constructivism shows how pupils make sense of what happens to them by actively 'constructing' the world for themselves. It dismisses the transmission model of learning – that knowledge could be conveyed to the pupil from some external source – instead, it posits, every individual has to create their own knowledge (von Glaserfeld 1987). For learning to take place, each pupil has to consciously reorganize his or her own current cognitive system to accommodate the new experience. If the new experience is too far outside the pupils' current framework, accommodation or assimilation cannot take place and the pupil will not acquire knowledge (Lerman 2000).

However, new experiences encountered by pupils in the classroom are almost always mediated, at least in part, by language within a social, cultural setting, and the role of language, community or the teacher are not clarified in constructivist theories.

> Because teachers and pupils each construct their own meanings for words and events in the context of the on-going interaction, it is readily apparent why communication often breaks down, why teachers and pupils frequently talk past each other. The constructivist's problem is to account for successful communication.
>
> (Cobb 1988, p. 92)

Socio-cultural theories place language at the heart of learning, as language is the main mediator of social interaction. Vygotsky (1962), Wertsch (1985), Bruner (1996) and Wood, Cobb and Yackel (1995) all discussed how children learn to take their place within society through the mediation of more competent peers using tools and signs, many linguistic, that are part of the social world. That is, that children develop 'higher mental functions' (Vygotsky 1981, p. 162) through social interactions that take place predominantly, but not exclusively, in verbalized language. For socio-culturalists, learning is construed as an individual becoming more able to take his place within a culture, or becoming enculturated, through social practices. Approaches in a classroom must therefore allow individuals to develop their own individual learning through being involved in developing knowledge within a community. According to socio-cultural theories, pupils' developmental functions occur first between people as an interpsychological category and only subsequently as an intrapsychological category, as an internalized mental function (Vygotsky 1981). That is, such functions occur initially in a social environment when interacting with other people.

> It is necessary that everything internal in higher forms was external, that is, for others it was what it now is for oneself. Any higher mental function necessarily goes through an external stage in its development because it is initially a social function ... Any higher

mental function was external because it was social at some point before becoming an internal, truly mental function.

(Vygotsky 1981, p. 162)

Successful communication in a classroom is therefore vital to learning, and as language issues in mathematics can be a barrier to such communication it is vital that the teacher works to reduce those barriers. Social-culturist theories provide the impetus to consider ways to improve pupils' facility in using language in mathematics classrooms.

Successful communication builds a community of learners who develop a common voice and common knowledge (Wood and Yackel 1990; Mercer 2000; Daniels 2001). Building a community invokes the notions of communities of practice in social practice theory, in particular the ideas of Lave and Wenger (Lave and Wenger 1991, Wenger 1999). Lave and Wenger's conceptual framework of social practice theory arose from their work with apprentices. They looked at how individuals came to know about the practices within a community by a process of 'legitimate peripheral participation'. Such ideas do not readily transfer to the classroom. A pupil is learning mathematics within the community of the classroom, not learning to be a mathematics teacher or even learning to be a professional mathematician, although either may be the ultimate outcome for a few of the pupils. However, many of the notions inherent in social practice theory are important to building a learning community in a mathematics classroom. 'Knowledgeability is a function of who we are with, where we are, what we are acting on and with, and all the histories, emotions social and power relations embedded in these inter-related aspects of being' (Adler 2000, p. 35). Changing a person's knowledgeability involves interaction with the resources of a community and is dependent on their transparency for participants, and mediating objects need to be invisible if they are to support the visibility of the subject matter. Pupil-to-pupil discussion, for instance, is a resource of the community of the classroom and can be used to increase knowledgeability. In order to enable mathematical learning, the rules of discussion may be intended to be invisible, as the focus is on increasing knowledgeability in mathematics. However, if the rules of the mediating discussion are not being adhered to, the functioning of the learning group may become the visible feature and obscure the mathematical learning. In order to enable knowledgeability in mathematics, the pupils must first become knowledgeable in the rules of classroom discussion, which will then become invisible. This is true of many of the resources in the classroom. There is a complex interplay between visibility and invisibility of the resources needed for effective functioning of a learning situation. In order to increase access to the practice of learning mathematics, activities must be organized that enable the mediating objects – for example, use of mathematical language or of physical tools – to become invisible in order to make mathematical meaning visible to participants in the practice of learning mathematics.

The theories of Lave and Wenger also reveal more about the importance of talk in a learning situation. They describe two different types of talk: talking 'within' and 'about' a practice. Full participation in a practice implies being able to talk as one who is a full participator. In this context learning mathematics involves learning to talk like a mathematician, something that resonates with others' theories – for example, those of Mercer (1995), Pimm (1991) and Laborde (1990) – and also with Gergen's theory of social construction of identity. However, the distinction for Lave is of talking within (talking as part of doing) and talking about (reflecting on), and it is in becoming able to follow these conventions that knowledgeability occurs. The learner learns to talk as a full participator in the community by engaging in the practices of the community. Therefore, from this point of view, the discourse in the classroom is a learning tool but only when it actively involves the learner; the pupils themselves need to talk both within and about the practice of mathematics. It is important that pupils are encouraged both to talk within and about mathematical activities and to help pupils understand how to do that.

Social practice theory also shows that pupils come to the classroom as part of many diverse communities in which they have formed their identities and they have to reshape their identities as they participate in the community of the classroom. It is in this reshaping of identity that learning resides. In social practice theory (Wenger 1999), coming to know is never separate from becoming. Social practice theory deals with knowledge and learning in a way that connects cognition and identity through becoming part of a community. The problems of transfer of knowledge are in part explained by these theories, as knowledge is bound up in the community in which we find ourselves. It is hard to use mathematics in the community of the science lesson since knowing mathematics is bound up in being part of a community learning mathematics.

'Identities are constructed within a context of activity, pupils build an identity, that is a way that they explain themselves, within each community in which they participate' (Holland *et al.* 1998, p. 270). Enabling pupils to build an identity as someone who is able to use mathematical ideas to solve problems is an important aim for a mathematics classroom. Gergen (1995) considers that 'knowing' only exists as part of a community and that in order to be said to 'know' mathematics, one must occupy a discursive position that is accorded the standpoint of authority by the social community of mathematicians. 'The ideal position is not knowing that something is the case, but knowing how to produce language that will be accorded status' (Gergen 1995, p. 31). That is, an individual takes on the identity of a mathematician, someone who 'knows mathematics', by learning how to talk like a mathematician.

Assessment for Learning

The theoretical underpinning of Assessment for Learning or formative assessment is well expressed elsewhere, in particular in Black and William (1998a) and Black *et al.* (2003). However, here I wish to explore some of the ways that improving the pupils' ability to use language is an essential ingredient to effective use of Assessment for Learning.

A key component of formative assessment is the concept of *feedback*. Feedback is an essential feature in any system that seeks to manage change, whether in states of learning or otherwise. The vital feature of assessment that is formative is that the information is used; if the information does not actually change the level of a pupil's knowledge, skill or understanding, then the feedback is not formative. Therefore, if the pupils do not understand the language in which the information is expressed, there is no feedback. If pupils routinely take part in discourse in which meanings are developed and shared, the mechanism for feedback is facilitated and the pupils are able to move their learning forward.

A further theoretical underpinning of formative assessment comes from Sadler (1989), who pointed out that the core of the activity of formative assessment lies in the sequence of two actions. The first is the perception by the learner of a gap between a desired goal and the learner's present state (of knowledge, and/or understanding, and/or skill). The second is that action is taken *by the learner* to close that gap in order to attain the desired goal. This implies that first the learner has to understand evidence about the gap and then be able to take action on the basis of that evidence. The learner is the active participant in this process; making the complex links between the evidence of the gap, the selection between different courses of action that could close the gap and the subsequent learning activity. These arguments make it clear that the development of self-assessment is an essential feature of using formative assessment.

The processes of feedback, questioning and self-assessment do not take place effectively without shared meanings within a classroom. The pupils have to take the action to close gaps in their learning and they have to understand how to do so. If their understanding of the language that is routinely used in the classroom is poor or if they rarely take part in the meaning-making processes of the classroom they will not be able to take the role of self-efficacy that is demanded by formative assessment. Peer assessment makes demands on pupils' skill in using language in mathematics. They have to discuss, understand and assess others' work against set criteria. Peer assessment is such an effective Assessment for Learning tool because it develops pupils' ability to self-assess; that is, to understand the evidence about the current state of their knowledge, skills or understanding and how to take action to close the gap between their current state and their desired goal.

Research undertaken on formative assessment (Black *et al.* 2002, 2003) showed that there are close links between the way that formative assessment practice developed and the teacher's conception of his or her role. Deep changes both in teachers' perceptions of their own role in relation to their students and in the way that they viewed good classroom practice were often necessary before effective formative assessment practices could be said to be established. The key features of these changes were as follows.

- In order to enhance feedback between those taught and the teacher, new ways of pedagogy had to be developed. In particular, approaches were developed that increased the level of discourse in the classroom so that more information was available on the level of understanding, skill and/or knowledge that the pupils currently possessed and how to move learning forward. The teachers and pupils 'no longer had to guess'; information for appropriate action was available.
- The teachers changed their assumptions about approaches that would result in effective learning. In particular they came to know that the pupils must be actively involved in the learning process.
- In order to use the assessments made by both teacher and pupil formatively, the information gained had to be used to adjust subsequent learning activities and the pupil had to have some involvement in and control over this process.
- Assessment affects both the motivation and the self-esteem of pupils; it is a significant part of the development of the identity of a learner. Self-assessment has a significant part to play in enhancing both motivation and self-esteem.

An important message from the Assessment for Learning literature is that lasting change is not made quickly or simply. The deep changes in practice that were the result of the Kings Medway Oxfordshire Formative Assessment Project (KMOFAP) came about over a substantial period of time and with support from researchers and other teachers in the group (Black *et al.* 2003).

> The improvement of formative assessment cannot be a simple matter. There is no 'quick fix' that can be added to existing practice with promise of rapid reward. On the contrary, if the substantial rewards of which the evidence holds out promise are to be secured, this will only come about if each teacher finds his or her own ways of incorporating the lessons and ideas that are set out above into her or his own patterns of classroom work. This can only happen relatively slowly, and through sustained programmes of professional development and support. This does not weaken

the message here – indeed, it should be a sign of its authenticity, for lasting and fundamental improvements in teaching and learning can only happen in this way.

(Black and Wiliam 1998n p.15)

Perrenoud expresses a further important point both about formative assessment and about pupils' response to changes in teachers' practice.

A number of pupils do not aspire to learn as much as possible, but are content to 'get by', to get through the period, the day or the year without any major disaster, having made time for activities other than school work ... Formative assessment invariably presupposes a shift in this equilibrium point towards more school work, a more serious attitude to learning ... Every teacher who wants to practise formative assessment *must reconstruct the teaching contracts so as to counteract the habits acquired by his pupils.* Moreover, some of the children and adolescents with whom he is dealing are imprisoned in the identity of a bad pupil and an opponent.

(Perrenoud 1991 p. 92, my italics)

Pupils may be reluctant to participate in any change, not merely from a wish to minimize effort, but also from fear and insecurity. A further issue could be that pupils fail to recognize formative feedback as a helpful signal and guide (Tunstall and Gipps 1996). The pupils' own beliefs about learning and their confidence in their own ability to be successful learners (Dweck 2000) have an enormous influence on their ability to become involved in the processes of learning. Therefore, careful building of the pupils' confidence to take part in the discourse of a mathematics classroom is an important tool in enabling them to use assessment formatively and enhancing their learning.

The mathematics classroom as a discourse community

Discourse is a learning tool

Discourse is acknowledged as an important tool in learning. 'The act of formulating ideas to share information or arguments to convince others is an important part of learning. When ideas are exchanged and subjected to thoughtful critiques they are often refined and improved' (NCTM 2000, p. 348). Asking pupils to articulate their ideas forces meta-cognitive activity and thus improves the clarity of their thinking. Research has shown that requiring pupils to share their mathematical thinking in lessons results in an increase in mathematical learning (Russell and Corwin 1991, Wood, Cobb and Yackel 1995). Discourse is important because making mathematics the subject of discussion in the classroom forces thoughts and ideas that may be tacit and latent to become the focus of attention. As the pupils formulate their own ideas in order to make them available for others, they make their thoughts overt and tangible for themselves.

Language is a tool through which pupils build their knowledge of mathematics, and knowledge is built in social settings (Vygotsky 1978; Wertsch and Toma 1995; Bruner 1996,). Viewing the interactions in the classroom as a discourse with the potential to enhance the social construction of knowledge 'shifts our focus from what is missing in the individual student's thinking to what is missing from their social interactions' (McNair 2001, p. 198). Discourse in the mathematics classroom should reflect an 'intentional effort to learn about a mathematics concept or procedure that has become problematic' (McNair 2001, p. 199). Further, if pupils stop short of discussing the procedures that, for example, are used to compute their answers they may not learn the mathematics embodied in those procedures (Lampert 1988, Walkerdine 1997); 'We learn to participate not only in activities but also in the meanings that inform them' (Barnes 1992 p. 128).

Pupils learn mathematics as they 'participate in the interactive constitution of the situations in which they learn' (Cobb *et al.*1992, p. 119). By participating in dialogic discourse in the classroom (Wertsch and Toma 1995), pupils negotiate any inconsistencies between their own and others' mathematical activity. In the dialogic function the discourse is a thinking device. Both the speaker and listeners take an active stance towards everything that is said by questioning and extending both the teacher's and their peers' utterances and 'incorporating them into their own external and internal utterances' (Wertsch and Toma 1995, p. 171).

A discourse community

Pupils learn effectively when teachers enable them to become part of a discourse community within the classroom, using language to build and express mathematical ideas, structuring the social context of the classroom so that the pupils use verbal and written language in the process of learning mathematics.

Silver and Smith use the name 'mathematical discourse community' to describe a classroom where

> the role of the teacher is diversified to include posing worthwhile and engaging mathematical tasks; managing the intellectual activity in the classroom including the discourse and helping pupils to understand mathematical ideas and to monitor their own under-

standing. Pupils are expected to engage in mathematics while participating actively in a 'discourse community'.

(Silver and Smith 1996, p. 20)

If the pupils are to engage in investigation and discourse about mathematical ideas and concepts then several conditions should be in place. Chief amongst these is an atmosphere of trust and respect. 'Unless the classroom environment is safe for thinking and speaking, pupils will be reluctant to propose their tentative ideas and hypotheses, to question assertions that are puzzling to them or to share their alternative interpretations' (Silver and Smith 1996, p. 22). It is important that the discourse in this 'safe' community must go beyond 'telling how you did it' or 'giving the answer'.

A mathematics classroom is a community convened for the complex practice of learning about mathematics. The learning and teaching of mathematics in school is a very specific social practice. It is a discursive community, or, more properly, a set of discourses, as there are many discourses that impinge on the classroom that are set in specific other social practices. The language that is used in the mathematics classroom is in part the mathematics register (Pimm 1987) but it also involves discourses from other communities such as pupils' social communities. When learning mathematics there are bridges to cross between the discourse routinely used in the classroom and the discourse of a wider mathematics community. These are significant and problematic. If the crossing between the discourse that pupils use in their own social setting and the discourse they are required to use in the mathematics classroom is too difficult, the pupil will be unable to take part in the discourse of the classroom.

Educated and educational discourse

Educational discourse is the discourse of teaching and learning in the classroom, the particular way of talking in a classroom. In a mathematics classroom the phrase 'Do exercise number 5' involves no more physical exertion than writing and thinking. All pupils engage to some extent in this discourse. Educated discourse in the case of mathematics classrooms may be thought of as the discourse of wider mathematical communities. It involves new ways of using language that enable pupils to participate in the discourse of wider communities who are acknowledged as educated in our society. In the mathematics classroom pupils become educated by becoming fluent users of the mathematics register for the purpose of communicating mathematical ideas.

The teacher's role is to enable pupils to participate in this educated discourse, and the problems of access and alienation that can be part of current mathematics education may be attributable, at least in part, to a failure to do this well.

the important goal of education is not to get students to take part in the conventional exchanges of educational discourse, even if this is required of them along the way. It is to get students to develop new ways of using language to think and communicate, 'ways with words' which will enable them to become active members of wider communities of educated discourse.

(Mercer 1995, p. 80)

Talking about their mathematical ideas enables pupils to have the opportunity to practise being users of educated discourse. The discourse of 'educated mathematicians' may not easily translate into the classroom, unless the teacher mediates the language and frames of reference of 'expert' discourse into the discourse of the classroom. 'The teacher's role is to translate what is being said into academic discourse, to help frame discussion, pose questions, suggest real life connections, probe arguments and ask for evidence' (Adler 1998, p. 174).

The pupils' participation in mathematical discourse, using the mathematical register, creates significant problems and challenges for a teacher. There is a need to create a pedagogy that focuses on these problems of participation in classroom discourse, the mathematical register and social situations, and ways to enable all to participate without the concomitant problems of alienation for some pupils.

Pupils in the classroom will be members of other communities which overlap with the mathematics classroom: the school, the family setting, the science lessons and so on. It is an empowering aim to encourage the discourse of the mathematics classroom to cross over into these other communities as well as the community of discourse that is the wider mathematics community. The business of the mathematics classroom is to work within the constraints and opportunities of other discourse communities in a way that facilitates the learning of mathematics. When pupils are able to think and communicate in these new ways of using language, that is the mathematics register, then they can be said to be using educated discourse. This is another way of thinking of someone who has learned mathematics.

Thinking and speech are intimately connected in the learning process

According to Sfard (2000, 2001), communication should not be viewed as a mere aid to thinking but 'almost tantamount to the thinking itself'. Communication and participation are linked; participation in a community demands communication with the other participants. Learning is first and foremost about the development of ways in which an individual participates in well-established communal activities, in this case in a mathematics classroom: 'Practices should be seen, therefore, as discursive formations within which what counts as valid knowledge is produced and within which what constitutes successful participation is also produced' (Lerman 2001, p. 100).

The desire to participate in discursive practices is one of the main motives for learning (Sfard 2001, p. 49). Thinking, speech and learning are linked in a complex representation of learning as participating in the discourse practices of a community that itself formulates meta-discursive rules that guide the general course of communication. Part of the teacher's role is to mediate the meta-discursive rules and thereby facilitate their students' participation in the community. Pupils come to know more as they struggle to communicate; communicating is thinking and discourse is a strong motivator in the learning process.

Changes in the teacher's and the pupils' role in a mathematical discourse community

One result of encouraging the pupils to use mathematical language more in their learning is that the more teachers engage their pupils in conversations, the better they come to know the pupils and the better the pupils come to know their teacher. The relationship changes markedly. Lessons become joint enterprises in the struggle to know and understand more about mathematics.

Teachers' relationships with their classes are often rather one-sided. Teachers maintain close control on what is said or done in the lessons, they try to find out or guess what would help their pupils learn more but do not expect the pupil themselves to have an opinion or to have insights into their own learning. The more teachers enter into a discourse with the pupils in the classroom, the more they become partners with their pupils in a joint venture to learn more about mathematics. Each pupil becomes a valued member of a learning community that talks about and shares their ideas about mathematics. The pupils in the class begin to take some of the responsibility for the constitution of the community and that enables the teacher to respond better to the learning needs of the pupils.

The teacher's role

The teacher's role in a discursive mathematics classroom is to enable the pupils to take ownership of the language that is used to express mathematical concepts. In order that the pupils should be able to use and control mathematical ideas they have to be able to articulate and discuss those ideas. Therefore much of the role of a mathematics teacher is to teach the pupils the meta-discursive rules of mathematical discourse (Sfard 2000). The teacher's role can be explained in this way:

> Most of the time the teacher may be considered as a representative of the cultural history of mathematics and in that quality the teacher should take part in the discourse in the classroom: not just as a guide when the process goes astray, but also as a participant, suggesting possible solutions strategies concepts etc.
>
> (Van Oers 2001, p. 74)

Therefore, teachers have many roles within a discursive mathematics classroom: planning questions and activities that will facilitate the pupils understanding, listening and assessing that understanding, and so on. However, one of the most important roles is that of participant in a meaning-making discourse, enabling the pupils to use the ways of expression that are particularly mathematical and to take part in the learning discourse. The teacher should model ways of using mathematical language so that the pupils know how it is used and also set up activities that demand the pupils' use of mathematical words and expressions. The teacher's role is to enable the pupils to know that they have learned to use and control mathematical ideas and this is achieved when the pupils can articulate and discuss those ideas themselves.

The teacher's role changes in overt and more subtle ways when they use mathematical discourse as a way to enable their pupils to learn mathematics. Teachers become part of the discourse and are therefore able to assess each individual's understanding and react to what they find more accurately. Assessment for Learning becomes totally embedded in the day-to-day business of the classroom. Teachers come to know their pupils well as they talk and learn together and they are able to plan to meet their actual learning needs and preferences. Teachers become more responsive to their pupils and know that they are teaching better, and they often gain more satisfaction from their job.

> I enjoyed classroom teaching again ... I was not facing piles of marking. I was looking forward to being creative and to planning the next day ... I was focusing on the girls' understanding and not on their behaviour. I often found that once the understanding was there, the behaviour followed.
>
> (Gwen)

Thinking about discourse and discourse communities recontextualizes the role of the teacher. The teacher works within the discourse with which the pupil is already comfortable and provides ways for the pupil to enter into the educated discourse of the wider mathematics community.

> Teachers are expected to help their students develop ways of talking, writing and thinking which will enable them to travel on wider intellectual journeys, understanding and being understood by other members of wider communities of educational discourse.
>
> (Mercer 1995, p. 83)

Looking at the classroom as a discourse community means that the teacher has to be sure that everyone can take part in it with an understanding of the ways of communication used. The onus is placed on the teacher to ensure that the discourse community shares a set of common goals, that there is information and feedback as part of its practice and that everyone shares an understanding of the mathematical register that is the basis of its communication. Pupils come to the classroom with discourse developed in their own social setting, their own natural language. They cannot participate in the discourse of educated mathematicians without help, practice and encouragement. This requires the activities in a classroom to be constituted in a way that will allow each member to participate in the discourse, 'offering them access to a shared inheritance of mathematical images and ideas, language and symbolism and the uses for mathematics which humans have so far developed' (Pimm 1995, p. 11).

Taking a role of manager or facilitator of a discourse community demands profound changes in many teachers practice. These include:

- moving away from being dominated by the curriculum; coverage of the curriculum without understanding is pointless and may even be harmful
- changing their beliefs about pupils' learning capacities from fixed to incremental (Dweck 2000) – teachers must see their pupils as able to improve given the right help and support
- stimulating more talking and thinking among their pupils and, therefore, doing less of the talking themselves
- letting go of some of the control they had previously exerted over teaching and learning and allowing the pupils to assume an appropriate degree of responsibility for the process.

The pupils' role

It is important that pupils realize that their role has changed in the talking and learning mathematics classroom. They will no longer be required to be passive recipients of information, but will be active in the learning process. Pupils must take part in the discourse, offering their ideas and opinions. They must also take responsibility for their own learning, thinking and talking about what they are learning and how well they are learning it.

LIVERPOOL JOHN MOORES UNIVERSITY
LEARNING SERVICES

It will be easier for some pupils to take a full part in the discourse than for others. Some pupils do find talking in class much harder than others. Nevertheless, the pupils are being asked to articulate their mathematical ideas in order to help clarify, explore and consolidate those ideas and to make them available for assessment by the teacher and by the pupils themselves. The process is intended to help them learn, so pupils cannot be allowed to opt out of talking. Some pupils will need more support than others, perhaps by asking them to express their mathematical ideas in small groups first. Asking pupils to talk to a partner and then to the whole class can help those pupils who find speaking difficult. However, most pupils will take part in the discourse without pressure if the ethos of the classroom is right, all responses are valued for their contribution to a meaning-making discourse and pupils can easily see and hear one another.

Pupils find articulating their mathematical ideas difficult. However, when asked, most pupils recognize that articulating their ideas is important as it forces them to clarify their own ideas. Pupils find devising explanations very complicated and need to be supported in knowing how to use language appropriately so that other people can understand their ideas. It is important that teachers acknowledge that expressing ideas is difficult but that with support and encouragement it will become easier. As the pupils become more proficient at using language to explain their mathematical ideas they will find learning mathematics easier as well.

Along with the requirement for the pupils to do much of the talking in the classroom there is also a requirement for the pupils to do their share of the thinking. This is less straightforward than it sounds as the pupils are often not used to being asked to really think things through in their lessons. All the ideas that have been suggested in this book require the teacher to plan, explain and model the learning task, and they require the pupils to think. If a teacher has difficulty implementing some of the ideas then it may be that the pupils are not used to their new role and all the thinking that it requires.

When the pupils are talking and thinking about their mathematical learning then they will be able to take responsibility for it. The pupils will be able to express when they are learning well and need to engage in deeper or broader learning. They will also be able to tell their teacher if they are having difficulty and need to slow down or to try another way to understand. The pupils are the ones that have to do the learning, therefore they must be expected to reflect on it and express their success and how they will continue to improve.

In a discourse community, pupils:

- take a considerable part in the process of learning – they become aware of their learning goals and how they can meet them

- participate in shared learning – all pupils are involved in a learning discourse with their peers
- become more confident and effective communicators
- learn to work in, and help to create, an ethos in which expressed misunderstandings are received empathetically as part of the discourse of learning.

A discourse community is a shared learning environment. This is how one teacher expressed it:

> We all had to be aware of everyone else, be prepared not just to listen, but to listen with an empathetic ear, we all had to understand and invest in a common goal, which was to move learning forward ... students felt safe to give wrong answers and to express, freely, their lack of understanding ... the classroom ceased to be a habitat where only the brightest survived and flourished, but one where, with careful grouping and good questioning, every student could feel themselves making progress through a lesson.
>
> (Robert)

The pupils' role in a discourse community is to take part. The teacher's role is to enable them to take part because they know that learning resides in participating. As the pupils form their ideas into language that can be shared, they change ideas that are transitory and indistinct into organized and more stable ideas, which is in itself part of the learning process. The sharing of ideas also makes them available to be compared against other ideas and possibly reformed into ones that are more useful for solving mathematical problems; in sharing, misconceptions are challenged and incomplete thought processes refined.

Changing practice

To conclude this chapter on the theoretical basis of the changes described in the rest of the book I want to look at some theory concerning teachers changing their own practice. Many of the ideas described were initially developed through action research, which is a very powerful way of changing practice. The ideas were then validated through work with other teachers who used the support of peers to develop their own understanding of a 'talking and learning' mathematics classroom. Therefore, all the changes advocated are the result of professionals seeking to improve their practice.

Sustained changes in practice happen when teachers' beliefs about what constitutes good practice are challenged and when they have the opportunity, time and support to explore for themselves what changes are necessary in the 'messy real world of practice' (Griffiths 1990, p. 43). It seems that many of the recent initiatives, for example the National Curriculum and the National Numeracy Strategy, have had the effect of providing a recipe for action which has not prompted the professional practice of reflection (Dewey 1938, Schön 1991). If the professional knowledge and values of teachers are to be extended or developed it will be because they discern the gap between their own current practice and the values they hold as part of the view they have of themselves as professional teachers (Whitehead 1989; Atkin 1992). Teachers need a facility to work out the meaning of the changes in practice *for themselves* (Fullan 1991, p. 112); only then will changes in ideas and processes become part of the teacher's own thoughts and beliefs about good practice. A suitable facility would be a community of like-minded individuals. Through participating in such a community teachers would come to see themselves as 'teachers who have developed their practice' (Holland *et al.* 1998, Wenger 1999) and deepen their knowledge of what it means to take on this identity. Participating in such a group is part of the way that a change is wrought in to the values they hold as professional teachers (Elliott 1987; Hargreaves 1998) and, therefore, part of the process of change in the intentions that drive the action of the teachers in a given situation.

Changing practice through action research

Action research provides a mechanism for professionals to explore their own practice. Teachers undertaking action research are in a privileged position when it comes to researching, analysing data and creating theory. Teacher researchers cannot enter their field of research in an unprejudiced manner (unlike sociologists, who might enter fields with which they are unfamiliar) because they already live and work in it. Prejudices acquired through their experience provide a motivation to explore and much relevant knowledge of the situation and interests with regard to further development. Rather than disregarding these 'prejudices', teacher researchers take them into account, use them, elaborate on and revise them by their research (Altrichter and Posch 1989, p. 26).

My 'prejudices' as I entered the field were that my pupils did not seem to learn mathematics as well as they did, say, geography or technology. Both geography and technology shared some of the 'barriers' to learning that seemed to me to be traditionally ascribed to mathematics; for example, technical language that encompassed large concepts and algorithmic ways of solving problems. Both subjects seemed better at enabling their pupils to overcome these barriers than I was in teaching mathematics. I reflected on geography lessons and it seemed to me that the pupils used language a great deal more to express their ideas. I reflected on technology lessons and it seemed to me that the pupils had far more control over the direction of their learning. Such innate prejudices had built up in me over time so that when I came to the theory expressing the need for pupils to use language to gain control over mathematical ideas, I was ready with ideas and experiences that enabled me to take these ideas forward. My experience led me to respond to what I was reading; what I had to work out was the expression of that theory in the practical realities of the classroom.

It can be difficult for professionals using action research to distance themselves from the data, which is their own practice. Teachers undertaking action research act in two distinct modes. In one mode they are the reflective teacher asking questions of their practice in order to improve the experience of their pupils. In the other mode, they are a researcher posing questions as to what could be the (implicit) meaning behind deciding to act in one way or another and how this can be made transparent. In order to provide some distance, professionals can attempt to separate the two roles, the theoretical background can be set out and the data collection planned as a researcher. Planning lessons that take account of the theoretical background must be done as a teacher (a 'reflective teacher' prepared to take time to reflect on her actions and to decide on further action based on those reflections, but still a teacher), as must considering the learning implications of these lessons and what to do next. Field notes or journals are the province of both the teacher and the researcher as they may not be written at all if the teacher were not a researcher but the teacher-researcher has access to and is able to reflect on the intentions and implications of the action. As the data are being generated, the teacher is in control of the situation and the priorities of the teacher take precedence. However, at a different level, the researcher-thinker is recording incidents, asking questions, provoking situations and learning what it was possible to do in a classroom. As the data collection is planned or the data analysed the discipline of the researcher takes precedence, but at the analysis stage the practitioner-thinker provides insights, stays the too-ambitious hand and learns from what is uncovered. 'In this way [that is, moving from teaching to research] an increasing objectivity is achieved that allows the researcher to declare her relationship to the data, so that the emotional involvement is not lost but is acknowledged as part of the "event" being researched' (Hatch and Shiu 1998, p. 308).

Action research cannot be undertaken lightly; it is a major time commitment, especially when undertaken as part of a group of like-minded individuals. The final report takes a great deal of this time but it is an important factor of the research, partly because research is 'systematic enquiry made public' (Stenhouse 1980), but also because the report, in whatever form it takes, makes tangible for the teacher and for others all the ideas that have been learned as part of the project. Action research is recognized as a powerful way to develop practice and there are schools that fund teachers to undertake such projects and give them time to do so as part of their

Continuing Professional Development programme. Some teachers will continue to fit researching and developing their practice into their already busy schedule, but if this is to be more widespread then time and resources will need to be provided more systematically.

Conclusion

This chapter has detailed some of the theory behind the changes in practice discussed in the final chapter. Theory is important to changing professional practice; teachers will always be taking a risk when they make changes and therefore need to be convinced that the changes they make will result in a better learning environment for their pupils. The literature is clear: thinking and language are intimately connected. Pupils learn to use and control mathematical ideas through using language to express those ideas, articulation forces the thinking to become less transitory and to become focused and clear. However, using mathematical language has another powerful effect: as pupils *talk like* mathematicians they take on the identity *of* mathematicians. That is, when pupils learn to be able to express their mathematical ideas in the same way as 'educated' mathematicians they come to see themselves as being 'educated', they are able to 'do' mathematics.

When the pupils are able to articulate their mathematical learning, both the learner and the teacher can make effective use of Assessment for Learning, moving learning forward as efficiently as possible. The classroom becomes a discourse community where the discourse is about learning mathematics; that is, the pupils discuss both the ideas they are learning and how well they are learning those ideas. The teacher and the pupil take on particular roles in a discourse community; the teacher does not dictate but manages and facilitates the learning. The pupil becomes active in the learning process, doing a great deal of the thinking and the talking, and takes on responsibility for their own learning.

When teachers become convinced that changes in their practice are necessary they must seek effective ways to make and establish those theoretical changes. Action research allows changes to be implemented, reviewed and reflected on and to become an embedded and sustainable part of professional practice.

7 Looking at practice more deeply

The ideas contained in this book are aimed at improving the learning environment in mathematics classrooms. This involves changes in the way that lessons are conducted and I have shown what this will entail, and discussed how such change can be made and why it is important. In this final chapter I explore more deeply the central idea of the book, discourse communities, and discuss how teachers can be supported in the difficult process of change.

A discourse community

A classroom that is a discourse community is a place in which pupils can learn mathematics as effectively and efficiently as possible. A classroom becomes a discourse community by building relationships of trust and respect between all members of the community of the classroom, pupil to pupil, pupil to teacher and teacher to pupil. The traditional roles of passive pupil and dictatorial teacher are abandoned and replaced with active pupils who express the ideas that they are coming to know and a teacher who manages the pupils' learning experience. Learning mathematics demands that pupils learn to think in a different way, a more abstract and systematic way, and learn how to communicate that thinking. As pupils communicate their thinking they come to know the extent to which they know, can do or understand mathematical ideas. Therefore, the teacher has to create a classroom where the pupils do most of the thinking and much of the talking as they learn to take a full part in a community that shares meanings and builds mathematical knowledge.

When pupils articulate their knowledge they organize their thoughts and become able to control and use mathematical ideas. Pupils have to learn to use the mathematics register in order to articulate their mathematical ideas effectively. The mathematics register enables the pupils to 'name' mathematical concepts, which allows them to conjure the meaning or interconnected web of ideas that the name denotes. When pupils express their ideas within a discourse community, they contribute to and share in a complex system of meanings that are generated by the community. Pupils who share in those meanings and are able to articulate them, begin to see themselves as people who know about mathematics. They come to see themselves as knowledgeable, taking on the identity of someone who can use and control mathematical ideas.

There are many discourses in a mathematics classroom. The most important are the pupils' own natural discourse, the 'educational' discourse which is the discourse that the pupils use as a tool to learn mathematics, and 'educated' discourse which is the discourse that would be used by those who are 'educated' in mathematics – that is, the mathematics register. There is a further discourse, which I have termed the conventional mathematical style, which is used to efficiently communicate mathematics. The conventional mathematical style is impersonal, atemporal and non-redundant; it uses the passive voice and strives for concision. These features of the conventional mathematical style make it very difficult for pupils to use. The mathematics register is not the conventional mathematical style, but it does use the mathematics register to convey mathematical meanings. It is not vital that the pupils use the conventional mathematical style to express their mathematical ideas and indeed the complexities of the style may well present a barrier to pupils learning mathematics. However, pupils may be disadvantaged if they are not able to use the conventional mathematical style to some extent because:

- part of being able to 'do' mathematics is to be able to express ideas concisely and logically and to use symbolic language effectively
- pupils need to take a part in the discourse of the wider mathematical community; to be able to do this effectively a person must be able to use the conventional mathematical style to an appropriate degree
- pupils must be able to understand the conventional mathematical style as it is used in examinations and it may help if they can use it themselves for assessed pieces of coursework.

Teaching can be seen as inducting the pupils into a community of mathematical knowledge. Mathematical education is drawing children into a new sphere of understanding, a process of re-acculturation in which a student moves from one culture to another: 'In the school context doing and learning mathematics means improving one's abilities to participate in mathematical practice both the operational part (the symbolic technology of mathematics) and the discursive part' (Van Oers 2001, p. 72).

Seeing mathematics education as increased participation in a new culture or community re-emphasises how complex and difficult the process is for pupils. Enculturation emphasises the importance of learning to participate in the discourse *at the same time as* learning to participate in the symbolic technology of mathematics. Mathematics can be viewed as coming to use a second language that has to be learned in context (Usiskin 1996). Participating in this new culture means that the pupils have to take ownership of the words, rather than replicate their teacher's words. In order to help pupils share in the culture or community of mathematics, teachers have to use approaches in the classroom that increase pupils' ability to participate in the discourse. Pupils take part in a creative meaning-making process and try out their expectations of meaning or initiate new meanings as part of a process of 'becoming' part of the community.

Identities are formed and re-formed through participation in a community. Discursive practices allow pupils to form an identity as a successful learner of mathematics or to become successful participators in a community of people developing their ability to use and control mathematical ideas. 'Social practices are discursively constituted and people become part of practices as practices become part of them' (Lerman 2001, p. 88). Troy radically changed the way that he presented himself in the classroom, from negative and disinclined to solve mathematical problems, to a positive participatory stance. As he took part in the discourse he formed and reformed his identity as the practices he was part of became part of him. Chantelle also redefined her identity as she became part of the discourse community.

Chantelle
Chantelle was described as 'fairly bright' but did not work 'unless forced to' at the start of the project. She found settling to work very difficult as she always had something else to chat about other than her mathematics. She did not think about the meanings of the words that she was confronted with, and she could not equate the phrase 'square numbers' in her textbook with 'the number squared' that we had talked about in class. I had written that *'I did not talk about square numbers particularly but many of them made the transition from 4 being "two squared" to 4 being "a square number". Not all – Nina and Chantelle asked about it.'*

Chantelle slowly started to take more part in the discussions in the lesson and started to use discourse to move her learning forward. She was working in a small group exploring packages for golf balls when I recorded this exchange:

'How will you fit the golf balls in here Chantelle?' I said, pointing to a square-based pyramid. 'Two side by side and one on top?' she said hesitantly, 'So is a square the best shape?' 'No, it should be a rectangle, I'll change that.'

Chantelle followed up this conversation with a great deal of work at home; expressing her ideas aloud had enabled her to see the flaw in her thinking and to have the confidence to really explore her ideas. She realised that she could be successful with her work and therefore was prepared to make the effort required to complete it well. From this time on I saw a marked change in her attitude to mathematics.

Chantelle began to play an important part in the discussion in the classroom. In a spreadsheets lesson I could rely on Chantelle to read and explain the instructions for the work: I noted that 'I got Chantelle to read one of the instructions, and explain how to write out the formula for the spreadsheet and to fill in the missing ones.' I would not have been able to ask her to do this at the start of the research period.

Chantelle made significant progress, she moved from negative and uninterested at the start of the project to willing and concerned to complete work of a high standard. She progressed from being an unreliable student, to being the one that I could count on to make a significant contribution to class discussion.

One pupil's participation in the discourse can enable others to participate. Some pupils are able to 'get things started' in a discourse community. The teacher's goal is to include everyone in the learning conversations but it is necessary to start somewhere. 'Interactions should not be seen as windows on the mind but as discursive contributions that may pull others forward into increasing participation in speaking/thinking in their zones of proximal development' (Lerman 2001, p. 89).

Collette

Collette enabled other pupils to enter into the discourse. She seemed prepared to hazard an opinion or statement before others in the class and her statements encouraged others to speak. Collette seems to have been able to interact with me, her teacher, in a way that enabled the others to participate within their zones of proximal development where increased participation, or learning, could take place.

Some pupils are less able to become part of the community than others. Some pupils cannot participate in a meaning-making community in the same way as the rest of the class. They are not excluded from the community but they do not participate as fully as the other members of the class. The literature on discourse communities explains their lack of participation in two ways. The pupils may have had historical reasons why they developed an identity as a non-conformist as a result of the way that the community developed. 'Non-conformity is consequently not just a feature of the way that an individual might react as a consequence of her or his own goals in a practice or previous network of experiences but also of the practice itself'

(Lerman 2001, p. 100). The other explanation is that communication failed with these pupils, either that they failed to make meaning from others' communication or that the failure was a function of the community itself (Zack and Graves 2001, pp. 263–5).

Shaun
Shaun saw himself as a non-conformist. He was 'one of the lads' and he acted in a spontaneous way in the classroom, not listening to others or thinking about their contributions. Shaun did not have the social skills to participate in a discourse community. He would need special help in order to understand the demands of a discourse community, to listen to others and use their understandings to build his own knowledge.

Key characteristics of a discourse community

Classrooms that are discourse communities display the following characteristics.

Every member of the community has the opportunity to contribute to the discourse. A discourse community develops insofar as each member articulates their ideas and shares what they know or have discovered. The pupils will be helped to learn mathematics by taking as full a part as possible in the community. Therefore, every voice is valued for its contribution to the discourse.

The community makes and shares meanings and develops knowledge. The discourse of the community enables meanings to be developed for the words and phrases used. These meanings are shared within the community and, therefore, every member learns to know the web of interconnecting ideas and concepts that are associated with the words and phrases used within the community. The teacher also shares in these meanings and can act to correct misconceptions or misdirections.

The community has an atmosphere of trust and respect. Everyone in it takes an appropriate responsibility for the learning that goes on therein. An important facet of a discourse community is that the members listen carefully and respond to one another. When a teacher models acting in this way and encourages the pupils to do the same she helps to build an appropriate atmosphere. As the pupils begin to feel themselves a part of the classroom community they also begin to take on some responsibility for the actions within it. The locus of control shifts, the pupils take control over such things as how long they spend on activities and begin to see that they should act as teachers when they are able to do so.

The community is related to the identities of those within it. As the pupils became better able to take part in the discourse of the community their perception of themselves changes. The pupils' developing ability to articulate their ideas about mathematics leads them to begin to see themselves as having learned some mathematics and as able to learn more.

Changing practice

Changes in practice happen when teachers come to know that there are different ideas or ways to act within the classroom that may improve the way that their pupils learn, are able to engage with those ideas, and have the time, motivation and support to find out what those changes mean in terms of those practices. First, I discuss the term 'theorised practice', which describes and explains how professionals engage with ideas or theory and make them their own, then I examine how teachers can be supported so that they can make sustained changes.

Theorised practice

Theorised practice is the name I give to changes in practice that are the result of professionals using theory to guide changes in their own practice and further develop that theory. Such changes demand that the teacher's beliefs about what is 'good' teaching change and therefore have the potential to be sustained. Changing professional practice demands theoretical underpinnings. Theories 'in use' in professional practice often derive from tacit understanding (Arygis and Schön 1974, Torff 1999). Many professionals are unaware of the sources of their professional knowledge and are unable to give a straightforward description of it (Altrichter *et al.* 1993). However, as teachers seek to improve their practice they begin to make overt the theory that is guiding those changes and become part of the complex interplay between theory and action – theory driving changes in practice and practice exemplifying and extending theory. It is in this interplay that theory has the potential to become personalised as a belief system and thereby sustains lasting changes in practice. I call the results of this dialectic interplay between theory and practice, 'theorised practice'.

The synthesis of theory and practice which I call theorised practice is more than a process of critical reflective thinking (Schön 1983) and is more closely mirrored in the concept of *praxis*.

> In praxis, thought and action (or theory and practice) are dialectically related. They are to be understood as mutually constitutive as in a process of interaction which is continual reconstruction of thought and action in the living historical process which evidences itself in every real social situation. Neither thought nor action is pre-eminent ... In praxis the ideas which guide action are

just as subject to change as action is, the only fixed element is phronesis, the disposition to act truly and rightly.

(Carr and Kemmis 1986, p. 34)

Theorised practice requires a close relationship between thought and action, with one reconstructing the other. Pre-eminence of thought or action changes during the process – at the start thought may take precedence as studying theory or others' practice changes thinking about teaching, but, as the change process proceeds, the action in the classroom takes over. Changes in the way that teachers make split-second decisions or respond to their pupils' perceptions are the result of internalizing theory. Changes in the way that pupils respond to the planned activities change the way teachers think about their teaching.

Engaging with the theory explained in this book may change teachers' beliefs about how to act in a classroom, demanding that their pupils are involved in their work and can talk freely about mathematical concepts. These become theorized actions, approaches that teachers begin to consider must be present in a classroom, although the details will be changed to suit the situation and the topic. These theorized actions are theorized practice, in which thought and action are mutually constitutive but are also distinct and expressible, at least in part. Theorized practice embodies all the complexities, unruliness and untidiness of practice, along with the recognition that theory can and should be part of practice but can never fully explain it. Professionals use practice to understand theory and use theory to make sense of practice.

Sustained change

There are many ways that teachers come to know that their practice must change but if those changes are to be sustained then certain factors have to be in place. Sustained change has to be the result of teachers' belief systems changing through the processes of theorized practice. It happens when teachers have the following.

1 *Credible evidence* The strongest motivating factor for change is credible evidence that the changes advocated will make a difference to the pupils' achievement. Teachers are under a great deal of pressure as a result of the work that they do and they will not make changes unless they are sure that those changes will result in increased learning for their pupils.

2 *Practical ideas* An important element in making changes in practice are practical strategies that can be used immediately. Inevitably, these are sometimes used rather mechanistically by some teachers at first and change is slow to begin with, but the

success of these simple starting points gives teachers confidence to adapt and modify them and, later, to generate their own ideas. The process of theorised practice starts for some teachers with the theory, but for many it starts with practice – seeing ideas work and reflecting on why they work and how they may be made even more successful.

3   *Support* The support of working as part of a professional learning community is, if not essential, then at least highly desirable if the ideas are to become embedded in teachers' practice. Teachers value the motivation of a 'community of like-minded individuals' in beginning the process of engaging with ideas and in providing structure to their exploration of changes. Action research groups that have been formed in some schools or as part of a Higher Education Institute provide both motivation, support and structure as teachers seek to change their practice.

4   *Reflection on, in and about action* Support from peers in school or elsewhere also prompts both immediate reflection on action and deeper reflection that can provide new insights and perspectives. The sharing of information and collegiality of responding to it provide a supportive environment for sustained reflection about action.

5   *Time* Changing teachers' thinking and practice takes a long time. In the KMOFAP project (Black *et al.* 2003) although the teachers' thinking had clearly been influenced by what they had heard about the research and the associated strategies, it took a long time to integrate these new ideas into their practice. Indeed, in January 2000 – almost a year into the project – only modest changes in classroom practice could be observed and it would have been tempting at that point to conclude that something different was needed. However, a few months later, things appeared to 'fall into place' for many of the teachers, and radical changes in classroom practice could be seen.

It is very difficult for teachers to find the time to talk and think about changes in their practice in school. Unless time is specifically allocated for the purpose, the other demands of school life usually get in the way. Of course, the determined few do find the time and practice is explored and changes made. However, schools that wish to support their teachers in developing their teaching and learning practice should specifically set aside time for this important enterprise.

6   *Flexibility* Much teacher professional development seeks to 'tell teachers what to do'. However, unless teachers receive flexible support in integrating new ideas into their existing practice, then any changes produced tend to be minor and transient. Teachers are

in the difficult situation of having to maintain the success they obtained with their old strategies while developing new practices at the same time. Teachers who can decide which approaches to try, and the rate at which they try them, maintain ownership of the process and this is crucial for success.

The end – or the beginning?

Mathematics is empowering – those people who know that they can use mathematics can and do take control of aspects of their lives in ways that people who feel they are not able to 'do' mathematics cannot. This book has been about ways that learners can see themselves as able to 'do' mathematics. A large part of this is to be able to talk about mathematical ideas. Pupils that talk about mathematics, using the mathematics register, know that they can use mathematical ideas. They can assess their learning accurately because they can articulate how successfully they have learnt the ideas so far and can use that assessment to guide further learning. Pupils who are enabled to talk about mathematical ideas think more about those ideas and their learning is more secure and accessible. They see the connections and links between areas of mathematics.

Talking about mathematical ideas also affects the self-esteem of pupils. As pupils become more able to use mathematical language and ways of expression they come to see themselves as mathematicians, people who can use mathematical ideas and concepts effectively to find answers and solve problems. They also come to see themselves as successful learners because part of the process of talking about mathematics is trying out ideas – sharing, comparing and reformulating concepts until they know that their conception accords with the learning goal. Pupils know *what* they have learned, *that* they have learned and begin to develop insight into *the way* that they learn. They come to think of themselves as successful learners of mathematics.

This book will have achieved its goal if it has helped teachers to think about the importance of the pupils talking and thinking more in mathematics lessons. Making any change is a risky journey and that is why I have included ideas about how teachers may be supported in making that change. Securing commitment is important, but sustained change comes with thought, reflection and review of practice. It is not impossible to make changes in isolation, but the support of like-minded individuals from school or the wider academic community can provide the motivation to keep going during the 'conscious incompetence' stage when teachers and their pupils are confused and upset by all the modifications that are being made.

The ideas in this book provide a starting point for a journey into practice where pupils and teacher work together to enable learning by developing a mathematical discourse within the community of the classroom. The particular details of what this means in a particular school with a particular class have to be worked out at each stage of the journey by the participants in the community. The principles in Chapters 2 and 6 and the practical considerations in Chapters 3, 4 and 5 work together to guide the journey, but the journey must be made with thoughtfulness and commitment. Success will not be instant; it will take time for both teacher and pupils to grow accustomed to their changed roles in the classroom – the teacher to managing the learning rather than directing or dictating, the pupils to thinking and articulating their thinking, and taking responsibility for their own learning.

In a talking and learning classroom, a discourse community, pupils will come to know that they can use and control mathematical ideas, that they can be mathematicians. Therefore, working with pupils in a way that enables them to think about and articulate their mathematical ideas will empower those pupils, they will know that they can use mathematics to find answers for problems that they encounter. They will find that they can 'do' mathematics.

References

AAIA (2003) *Self-assessment*. AAIA website.

Adler, J. (1998) Lights and limits: recontextualising Lave and Wenger to theorize knowledge of teaching and learning of school mathematics. In *Situated Cognition and the Learning of Mathematics*, edited by A. Watson. Oxford: University of Oxford Department of Educational Studies.

Adler, J. (2000) Social practice theory and mathematics teacher education. *Nordic Studies in Mathematics Education* 8(3).

Altrichter, H. and Posch, P. (1989) Does the 'Grounded Theory' approach offer a guiding paradigm for teacher research? *Cambridge Journal of Education* 19(1): 21–31.

Altrichter, H., Posch, P. and Somekh, B. (1993) *Teachers Investigate their Work: an introduction to the methods of action research*. London: Routledge.

Arygis, C. and Schön, D. (1974) *Theory in Practice*. San Francisco: Jossey-Bass.

Atkin, J.M. (1992) Teaching as research: an essay. *Teaching and Teacher Education* 8(4): 381–90.

Barnes, D. (1992) The role of talk in learning. In *Thinking Voices*, edited by K. Norman. London: Hodder & Stoughton.

Black, P. and Wiliam, D. (1998a) Assessment and classroom learning. *Assessment in Education* 5(1): 7–74.

Black, P. and Wiliam, D. (1998b) *Inside the Black Box*. London: Kings College.

Black, P., Harrison, C., Lee, C., Marshall, B. and Wiliam, D. (2002) *Working Inside the Black Box – Assessment for Learning in the Classroom*. London: NfER.

Black, P., Harrison, C., Lee, C., Marshall, B. and Wiliam, D. (2003) *Assessment for Learning – Putting it into Practice*. Buckingham: Open University Press.

Bruner, J. (1996) *The Culture of Education*. Cambridge, MA: Harvard University Press.

Butler, R. (1988) Enhancing and undermining intrinsic motivation: the effects of task-involving and ego-involving evaluation on interest and performance. *British Journal of Educational Psychology* 58: 1–14.

Carr, W. and Kemmis, S. (1986) *Becoming Critical, Education, Knowledge and Action Research*. Lewes: Falmer Press.

Cazden, C. (1986) Classroom discourse. In *Handbook of Research on Teaching*, edited by M. Wittrock. New York: Macmillan.

Clarke, S. (2005) *Formative Assessment in the Secondary Classroom*. London: Hodder Arnold.

Cobb, P. (1988) The tension between theories of learning and instruction. *Educational Psychologist* 23(2): 87–103.

Cobb, P., Yackel, E. and Wood, T. (1992) Interaction and learning in mathematics classroom situations. *Educational Studies in Mathematics* 23(1): 99–122.

Cockcroft, W.H. (1982) *Mathematics Counts*. London: HM Stationery Office.

Daniels, H. (2001) *Vygotsky and Pedagogy*. London: Routledge Falmer.

DES/WO (1988) *Mathematics for Ages 5 to 16*. London: HMSO.

Dewey, J. (1938) *Logic: The Theory of Inquiry*. New York: Henry Holt.

DfES. (1989) *Mathematics in the National Curriculum*. London.

Durkin, K. and Shire, B. (1991) *Language in Mathematical Education Research and Practice*. Buckingham: Open University Press.

Dweck, C. (2000) *Self Theories: their role in motivation, personality and development*. Lillington, NC: Psychology Press, Taylor & Francis

Elliott, J. (1987) Educational theory, practical philosophy and action research. *British Journal of Educational Studies* 35(2): 149–69.

Elliott, J. (1991) *Action Research for Educational Change*. Milton Keynes: Open University Press.

Ervynck, G. (1992) Mathematics as a foreignlanguage. Paper read at PME, at Durham NH.

Evans, J. and Tsatsaroni, A. (1994) Language and subjectivity in the mathematics classroom. *Cultural Perspectives on the Mathematics Classroom*, edited by S. Lerman. Netherlands: Kluwer.

Fullan, M.G. (1991) *The New Meaning of Educational Change*. London: Cassell Educational Ltd.

Gergen, K.J. (1995) Social construction and the education process. In *Constructivism in Education*, edited by L.P. Steffe and J. Gale. Hove, UK: Lawrence Erlbaum Associates.

Griffiths, M. (1990) Action research: grass roots practice or management tool? In *Staff Development in Schools: an action research approach*, edited by P. Lomax. Clevedon: Multi-lingual Matters.

Halliday, M.A.K. (1975) Some aspects of sociolinguistics. In *Interactions between Linguistics and Mathematical Education*. Copenhagen: UNESCO.

Halliday, M.A.K. and Martin, J.R. (1993) *Writing Science: Literacy and Discursive Power*. London: Falmer Press.

Hardcastle, L. (1993) Do they know what we are talking about? *Mathematics in School* 22 (May).

Hargreaves, A. (1998) *International Handbook of Educational Change.* Dordrecht, the Netherlands: Kluwer Academic Publishers.

Hatch, G. and Shiu, C. (1998) Practitioner research and the construction of knowledge in mathematics education. In *Mathematics as a Research Domain: a search for identity*, edited by A. Sierspinska and J. Kilpatrick: Kluwer Academic Publishers.

Holland, D., Skinner, D., Lachicotte, W. and Cain, C. (1998) *Identity and Agency in Cultural Worlds.* Cambridge, MA: Harvard University Press.

Jaworski, B. (1994) *Investigating Mathematics Teaching.* London: Falmer Press.

Kluger, A.N. and DeNisi, A. (1996) The effects of feedback interventions on performance: a historical review, a meta-analysis, and a preliminary feedback intervention theory. *Psychological Bulletin* 119: 254–84.

Laborde, C. (1990) Language and mathematics. In *Mathematics and Cognition*, edited by P. Nesher and J. Kilpatrick. Cambridge: Cambridge University Press.

Lampert, M. (1988) *The Teacher's Role in Reinventing the Meaning of Mathematical Knowing in the Classroom.* Michigan: The Institute for Research on Teaching, Michigan State University.

Lave, J. and Wenger, E. (1991) *Situated Learning: legitimate peripheral participation.* Cambridge: Cambridge University Press.

Lee, C.S. (2004) *The Role of Language in the Learning of Mathematics.* DPhil, Educational Studies, Oxford.

Lerman, S. (2000) Some problems of socio-cultural research in mathematics teaching and learning. *Nordic Studies in Mathematics Education* 8(3): 55–71.

Lerman, S. (2001) Cultural, discursive psychology: a sociocultural approach to studying the teaching and learning of mathematics. *Educational Studies in Mathematics* 46: 87–113.

Mason, J. (2002) *Researching your own Practice, the Discipline of Noticing.* London: Routledge Falmer.

McNair, R. (2001) Working in the mathematics frame: maximizing the potential to learn from students' mathematics classroom discussions. *Educational Studies in Mathematics* 2000(42): 197–209.

Mercer, N. (1995) *The Guided Construction of Knowledge.* Clevedon: Multilingual Matters Ltd.

Mercer, N. (2000) *Words & Minds.* London: Routledge.

Morgan, C. (1995) An analysis of the discourse of written reports of investigative work in GCSE mathematics. PhD dissertation, Institute of Education, University of London, London.

Morgan, C. (1998) *Writing Mathematically.* London: Falmer Press.

Morgan, C. (1999) Convention or necessity? The impersonal in mathematical writing. Paper read at British Society for Research into Learning Mathematics, Coventry.

National Council of Teachers of Mathematics (1991) *Professional Standards for Teaching Mathematics*. Reston, VA: NCTM.

National Council of Teachers of Mathematics (2000) *Principles and Standards for School Mathematics*. Reston, VA: NCTM.

Otterburn, M.K. and Nicholson, A.R. (1976) The Language of (CSE) mathematics. *Mathematics in School* 5(5): 18–20.

Perrenoud, P. (1991) Towards a pragmatic approach to formative evaluation. In *Assessment of Pupils' Achievement: Motivation and School Success*, edited by P. Weston. Amsterdam: Swets and Zeitlinger.

Pimm, D. (1987) *Speaking Mathematically*. London: Routledge & Kegan Paul.

Pimm, D. (1991) Communicating mathematically. In *Language in Mathematical Education*, edited by K. Durkin and B. Shire. Buckingham: Open University Press.

Pimm, D. (1995) *Symbols and Meanings in School Mathematics*. London: Routledge.

Pimm, D. (1996a) Diverse communications. In *Communication in Mathematics K-12 and beyond*, edited by P.C. Elliott. Reston, VA: NCTM.

Pimm, D. (1996b) Plenary address to PME Conference. Paper read at 20th Conference of the International Group for the Psychology of Mathematics Education, at Valencia, Spain.

Potari, D. and Jaworski, B. (2002) Tackling complexity in mathematics teaching development: using the teaching triad as a tool for reflection and analysis. *Journal of Mathematics Teacher Education* 5: 351–80.

Russell, S.J. and Corwin, R.B. (1991) Talking mathematics: 'going slow' and 'letting go'. Paper read at 13th Annual Meeting of the North American Chapter of the International Group for the Psychology of Mathematics Education, Blacksburg.

Sadler, A.J. and Thorning, D.W.S. (1987) *Understanding Pure Mathematics*. Oxford: Oxford University Press.

Sadler, R. (1989) Formative assessment and the design of instructional systems. *Instructional Science* 18: 119–44.

Schön, D.A. (1983) *The Reflective Practitioner*. Aldershot: Avebury.

Schön, D.A. (1991) *The Reflective Practitioner*. Aldershot: Avebury.

Sfard, A. (2000) Steering (dis)course between metaphor and rigour: using focal analysis to investigate the emergence of mathematical objects. *Journal for Research in Mathematical Education* 31(3): 296–327.

Sfard, A. (2001) There is more to discourse than meets the ears: looking at thinking as communicating to learn more about mathematical learning. *Educational Studies in Mathematics* 46: 13–57.

Sherin, M.G. (2002) A balancing act: developing a discourse community in a mathematics classroom. *Journal of Mathematics Teacher Education* 5(3): 205–33.

Shuard, H. and Rothery, A. (1984) *Children Reading Mathematics*. London: John Murray Ltd.

Silver, E.A. and Smith, M.S. (1996) Building discourse communities in mathematics classrooms. In *Communication in Mathematics K–12 and Beyond*, edited by P.C. Elliot. Reston, VA: NCTM.

Stenhouse, L. (1980) Site lecture, at Simon Fraser University, Vancouver.

Tapson, F. (1997). Watch your mathematical language! *Mathematics in School* 26(1).

Torff, B. (1999) Tacit Knowledge in Teaching: folk pedagogy and teacher education. In *Tacit Knowledge in Professional Practice*, edited by R.J. Sternberg and J.A. Horvath. Mahwah: Lawrence Erlbaum.

Tunstall, P. and Gipps, C. (1996) Teacher feedback to young children in formative assessment: a typology. *British Educational Research Journal* 22(4): 389–404.

Usiskin, Z. (1996) Mathematics as a language. In *Communication in Mathematics K-12 and beyond*, edited by P.C. Elliot. Reston, VA: NCTM.

Van Oers, B. (2001) Educational forms of initiation in mathematical culture. *Educational Studies in Mathematics* 46: 59–85.

von Glaserfeld, E. (1984) An introduction to radical constructivism. In *The Invented Reality*, edited by P. Watzlawick. London: W.W. Norton & Co.

von Glaserfeld, E. (1987) Learning as a constructive activity. In *Problems of Representation in the Teaching and Learning of Mathematics*, edited by C. Janvier. Hillsdale, NJ: Lawrence Erlbaum.

Vygotsky, L.S. (1962) *Thought and Language*. Cambridge, MA: MIT Press New York.

Vygotsky, L.S. (1978) *Mind in Society* Cambridge, MA: Harvard University Press.

Vygotsky, L.S. (1981) The genesis of higher mental functions. In *The Concept of Activity in Soviet Psychology*, edited by J.V. Wertsch. Armonk, NY: M.E. Sharpe.

Walkerdine, V. (1997) Redefining the subject in situated cognition theory. In *Situated Cognition: Social Semiotic and Psychological Perspectives*, edited by K.D. and J. Whitson. Hillslade, NJ: Lawrence Erlbaum Associates.

Wenger, E. (1999) *Communities of Practice*. Cambridge: Cambridge University Press.

Wertsch, J.V. (1985) *Vygotsky and the Social Formation of Mind*. Cambridge, MA: Harvard University Press.

Wertsch, J.V. and Toma, C. (1995) Discourse and learning in the classroom: a sociocultural approach. In *Constructivism in Education*, edited by L.P. Steffe and J. Gale. Hove, UK: Lawrence Erlbaum Associates.

Whitehead, J. (1989) Creating a living theory from questions of the kind, 'How do I improve my practice?' *Cambridge Journal of Education* 19(1): 41–52.

Wood, T. and Yackel, E.R. (1990) The development of collaborative dialogue within a small group interaction. In *Transforming Children's Mathematical Education: International Perspectives*, edited by L.P. Steffe and T. Woods. Hillsdale, NJ: Lawrence Erlbaum.

Wood, T., Cobb, P. and Yackel, E. (1995) Reflections on learning and teaching mathematics in elementary school. In *Constructivism in Education*, edited by L.P. Steffe and J. Gale. Hove, UK: Lawrence Erlbaum Associates.

Zack, V. and Graves, B. (2001) Making mathematical meaning through dialogue: 'Once you think of it, the Z minus three seems pretty weird'. *Educational Studies in Mathematics* 46: 229–71.

Index

ASSESSMENT FOR LEARNING
Putting it into Practice

Paul Black, Chris Harrison, Clare Lee, Bethan Marshall and Dylan Wiliam.

"This is a surprising and welcome book... a heartening read that shows the power of assessment for learning and the potential for academics and teachers jointly to put into practice ideas that can improve classroom learning and teaching."

TES

The starting point of this bestselling book was the realisation that research studies worldwide provide hard evidence that development of formative assessment raises students' test scores. The significant improvement in the achievements of the students in this project confirms this research, while providing teachers, teacher trainers, school heads and others leaders with ideas and advice for improving formative assessment in the classroom.

Assessment for Learning is based on a two-year project involving thirty-six teachers in schools in Medway and Oxfordshire. After a brief review of the research background and of the project itself, successive chapters describe the specific practices which teachers found fruitful and the underlying ideas about learning that these developments illustrate. Later chapters discuss the problems that teachers encountered when implementing the new practices in their classroom and give guidance for school management and LEAs about promoting and supporting the changes.

This book offers valuable insights into assessment for learning as teachers describe in their own words how they turned the ideas into practical action in their schools.

Contents: *Introduction: Why study this book? – The source of the ideas – How teachers developed the ideas with us – Putting the ideas into practice – Looking at practice more deeply – Changing yourself – Management and support – The end – and a beginning – Glossary – References – Index.*

152pp   0 335 21297 2 (EAN: 9 780335 212972) Paperback

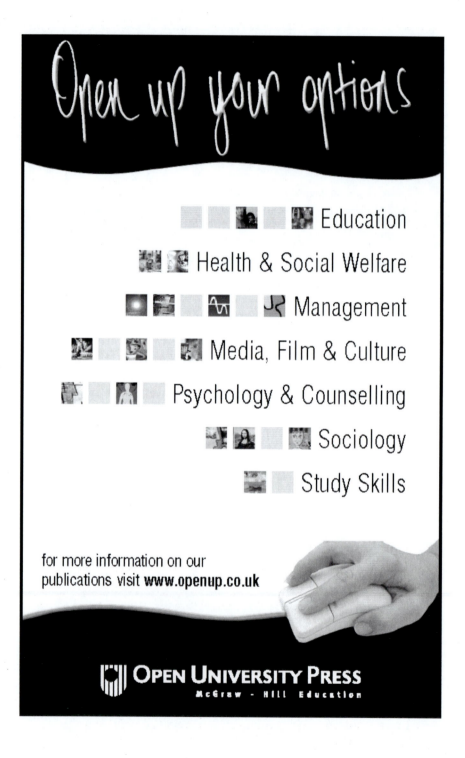

Open up your options

- Education
- Health & Social Welfare
- Management
- Media, Film & Culture
- Psychology & Counselling
- Sociology
- Study Skills

for more information on our publications visit **www.openup.co.uk**

OPEN UNIVERSITY PRESS
McGraw - Hill Education

Language for Learning Mathematics

LIVERPOOL JMU LIBRARY

3 1111 01383 7677

WITHDRAWN